Elegant HARDANGER *Embroidery*

YVETTE STANTON

Kangaroo Press

First published in Australia in 2002 by Kangaroo Press,
an imprint of Simon & Schuster (Australia) Pty Ltd
20 Barcoo Street, East Roseville NSW 2069

A Viacom Company
Sydney New York London

Visit our website at www.simonsaysaustralia.com

National Library of Australia
Cataloguing-in-Publication data

Stanton, Yvette.
   Elegant hardanger embroidery.

   Includes index.
   ISBN 0 7318 1096 1.

   1. Hardanger needlework. 2. Hardanger needlework – Patterns.
   I. Title.

746.44

Book design: Yvette Stanton
Typeset in Syntax 9.5 pt on 14 pt
Printed in Singapore by Kyodo Printing Co.

10 9 8 7 6 5 4 3 2 1

FOR EMMA AND JOHN

Contents

Introduction

Hardanger embroidery as we know it has evolved greatly from its origins in Persia and Asia, where it consisted of coloured silk embroidery worked on gauze fabric.

The technique travelled across Europe to the Hardanger Fjord region of south-west Norway. Because of the mountainous nature of this region it was geographically isolated, and so this style of embroidery developed independently and became quite distinctive. Local flax was used for the linen fabric and thread, and the technique became known as Norwegian drawn work. Traditionally white embroidery on white fabric, it was used for household linens and as decoration on folk dress.

To the novice, Hardanger may appear to be a difficult style of embroidery, but it is actually based on a small number of stitches which can be readily mastered. Hardanger embroidery requires only patience and the ability to count. If you can work counted embroidery then you can also do Hardanger.

This book features comprehensive, clear stitch instructions for beginners through to advanced Hardanger embroiderers. These techniques can then be used to create 15 beautiful projects, which are graded from beginner to intermediate and advanced.

The projects, with a range of household and decorative applications, feature traditional white on white embroidery. However, some take the technique further with the introduction of coloured fabrics and metallic, coloured and hand-dyed threads, as well as beading.

Some of the projects assume a knowledge of machine sewing and hand sewing practices, so a basic sewing kit and sewing machine are required for some of the projects.

Before you begin

Hardanger fabric

From top: Lugana (cotton/viscose blend), Hardanger fabric, even-weave linen

Hardanger embroidery is a counted thread embroidery requiring even-weave fabric. The most commonly used fabrics are even-weave linens, cottons and cotton/viscose blends. Aida cloth is not suitable for Hardanger embroidery.

Even-weave linen has a weave of single threads. Hardanger fabric, so called because it is used mostly for Hardanger embroidery, is made of a weave of double threads.

The "count" of an even-weave fabric refers to the number of threads per inch. Inches are used as the unit of measurement for the count of fabric, even in countries where metric measurements are standard. A 25 count fabric has 25 threads per inch, a 36 count fabric has 36 threads per inch, etc. The lower the count of the fabric, the larger the embroidery stitches will be.

To work out how large an embroidery will be on a specific count of fabric, you will need to know how many threads the embroidery will cover. If the embroidery is 100 threads square, on a 25 count fabric it will measure 4 inches or approximately 10 cm. On a 20 count fabric, the same design will measure 5 inches or approximately 12.5 cm.

To work out the size of the embroidery in inches, divide the number of threads covered, by the count of the fabric.

Traditionally, Hardanger is stitched in white thread on white cloth, but many designs are now made with coloured cloth or thread.

Thread

Hardanger embroidery uses two weights of thread. The heavier weight is used for satin stitching, and the lighter weight is used for all other stitching, including needle-weaving and eyelets. Occasionally a third, even lighter weight may be used for pulled thread work.

Pearl cotton (or perle coton) is the thread most often used for Hardanger. It is made of two strands twisted together and is indivisible (it cannot be split as it will fall apart). Pearl cotton comes in four different weights: Numbers 3, 5, 8 and 12. No. 3 is the thickest, and used only for very low counts of fabric. No. 12 is the thinnest, used for much finer work on higher counts of fabric.

The weight of the threads to be used is dependent on the count of the fabric. The heavier weight of thread must be able to provide good coverage of the fabric when sewn as satin stitch. Choose a weight that is similar to the thickness of the fabric's warp and weft threads.

The lighter thread to use in combination with the thicker thread would be the next weight down. For example, on 28 count fabric, use pearl cotton No. 5 for the satin stitching, and pearl cotton No. 8 for all other stitching.

Stranded embroidery cotton can also be used for Hardanger. Having a much wider range of colours available than pearl cottons, stranded cotton can be very useful. To create the two weights of thread needed,

Other equipment

NEEDLES

The needles used for Hardanger embroidery are tapestry needles. Tapestry needles have a round point which stops them from splitting the fabric threads. Because Hardanger is a counted embroidery, it is important that the stitches are worked in the spaces between the threads, and that the threads aren't split.

Some Hardanger embroiderers prefer to use two sizes of needle for their embroidery – a larger one for the thicker thread and a smaller one for the thinner thread. However, all the embroideries in this book have been done with the one size: a No. 24 tapestry needle.

SCISSORS

A pair of sharp, fine pointed embroidery scissors are essential equipment for Hardanger. They must be very sharp and fine to allow for the careful cutting of the fabric's threads very close to the embroidery, without cutting through the embroidered threads.

A pair of scissors that are not sharp or fine enough, or used incorrectly, can really make the difference between Hardanger embroidery that is executed to a high standard and Hardanger embroidery that is only average. It is worth investing in a quality pair.

EMBROIDERY HOOP

Some Hardanger embroiderers prefer to use an embroidery hoop while

different numbers of strands are used. For very fine needleweaving, a single thread of stranded cotton can produce very lacy results.

Before use, stranded cotton must always be "stripped": all the threads must be separated from each other and recombined. For two stranded work, remove one thread from the length to be used, by pulling it from the end of the six, and then another thread. The two threads are then put back together and used together. For six stranded work, all threads should still be separated. Stripping threads ensures that the strands lie flat when used and are less likely to twist around each other, producing a more pleasing result.

Embroidery threads come in a wide range of colours and are also available in metallics and hand dyed variegated colour schemes. They are most often 100 per cent cotton, but some varieties are silk, linen, wool, rayon, polyester or viscose, or a blend of fibres.

LENGTH OF THREAD

When stitching, I use approximately 80cm of thread. This length is easily measured out from skeins of pearl cotton by using the length of the skein as a guide. Take off the two paper bands and untwist the skein. Find an end and pull away a piece twice the length of the skein. Cut the piece off. It should be approximately 80 cm. When you are sure that this length suits you, cut through all the loops of one end of the untwisted skein so that all pieces are the same length.

If the length of thread you are using consistently becomes dull and furry before you have finished with it, it is too long and you should use a shorter piece.

Never re-use thread that you have unpicked. This thread will be noticeably less shiny than a fresh piece of thread and create an uneven visual effect in your work.

stitching. If you do choose to use one, make sure that the fabric is only loosely stretched across: if it is taut the satin stitches will buckle when the fabric rests again after removal from the hoop.

As a matter of personal preference, I choose not to use a hoop. Only one of the projects in this book was stitched using a hoop: the organza bolster. For this project it was essential for keeping the fabrics from slipping against each other while stitching. Experiment with and without the hoop to see what you prefer for your work.

Preparing your fabric for stitching

Before you begin, it is important to finish the edge of the fabric so that it doesn't fray as you stitch. To do this, either overlock the edge with a sewing machine or overlocker, or hand stitch with blanket stitch.

Once this is done, it is helpful to tack along both centre axes, carefully stitching over and under every four threads. Because Hardanger is worked on the basis of a four thread block, the counted tacking will help in the correct positioning of the stitching. Use pale coloured machine sewing thread, so that when it is removed it will not leave any dark fibres in the fabric.

To begin tacking, find the centre of the fabric by folding the fabric in half both ways. Mark the centre with a pin.

Enter the needle at the centre. Leave a tail of thread long enough to tack to the other edge. Bring the needle back up again after two threads. Weave over and under groups of four threads across to the edge of the fabric and secure the end of the thread.

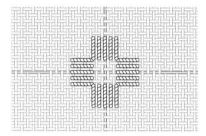

Using the long tail at the centre, begin tacking in the opposite direction with a stitch under two threads. Weave over and under

groups of four threads across to the other edge and fasten the end of the thread.

Repeat for the other centre axis.

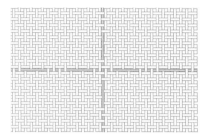

When working the embroidery, use the tacking to check that all stitches are in the correct place.

Remember to carefully remove the tacking stitches once the embroidery is finished.

Before you begin stitching, read through all instructions to give yourself an overview of how each of the steps fits together to create the finished stitch or project.

How to read a Hardanger chart

Like counted cross stitch, Hardanger is worked from a chart. There is no universally accepted notation for Hardanger charts, so different publications will show different symbols for stitches. Always refer carefully to the instructions and techniques before beginning to sew.

The chart below shows a centre kloster block grouping with an eyelet. Around this is an area of plain needleweaving, and then another row of kloster blocks.

The grid pattern denotes the fabric's threads. Each grid line corresponds to a thread in the fabric. The spaces between the grid lines denote the holes in the fabric.

The two lines with arrow pointed ends show the centre of the embroidery. These correspond with the tacked centre guides on your fabric. The second diagram shows how the pattern would look when stitched.

CREATING A FULL CHART

In this book, many of the charts in the projects chapter are not shown as full charts. Often just a half or a quarter of the chart is shown. When this is the case, the chart needs to be flipped and duplicated into the other half or quadrants.

A simple way to do this is to photocopy the section of the chart onto photocopier acetate and flip and rotate the design as needed. The flipped versions can also be re-photocopied onto paper and stuck together along the centre axes to create the full chart. You may find that this is not necessary if you are able to flip the chart in your mind's eye.

Pages 86–7 are a reference guide for chart symbols and their stitches.

In the stitch instructions chapter, underneath each instruction heading there are two diagrams showing

the chart symbol and how the stitch would appear when embroidered.

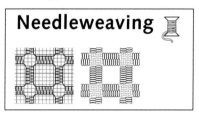

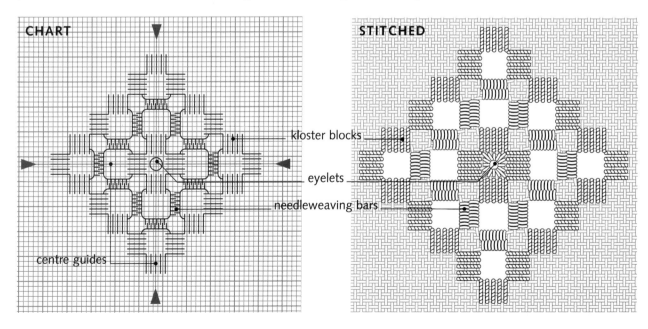

Left-handed Hardanger

Elegant Hardanger Embroidery can be successfully used by left-handed embroiderers.

All the project instructions are suitable for left-handed people. They need no allowances or changes to be made.

The stitch instructions will need to be reversed. The easiest way to do this is to substitute "right" wherever "left" is mentioned and vice versa. It may also help to reverse the diagrams. This can be done with the acetate method described in "How to read a Hardanger chart" (see left), or by holding the page up to a light source and looking at the diagram from the back of the page. You can also use a mirror to reverse the diagrams.

Left-handed embroiderers may encounter a few extra hurdles compared to right-handed people, but I am living proof that "lefties" can produce beautiful, high-quality embroidery that wins international embroidery awards!

Caring for embroidery

CARING FOR WORK IN PROGRESS

Always wash your hands before you begin your embroidery. It is also worthwhile to wash them periodically while you are stitching. The acids and oils on your hands will damage your work in the long term, so washing of hands is essential. While you may not see any damage in the short term, many invisible marks may become visible with time. Grubby hands and white on white embroidery do not mix!

Never leave your needle in the fabric at the end of your period of stitching. You cannot know how soon you will return to your work. In the meantime, the needle may begin to rust in the fabric, leaving a mark that can be very difficult to remove.

When you have finished each period of stitching, do not fold your work. Any crease in the fabric that is there for a long time will take an equally long time to come out. Ironing does not always remove stubborn creases. Instead of folding, roll your work up in a clean tea towel or pillowcase. This will also help to protect the work. Creases are also very likely to become grubby, so that if the crease is ironed out a mark may remain.

TO WASH OR NOT TO WASH

When the article is finished, you may decide to wash it. There are two schools of thought about washing needlework. Some say that you shouldn't do it, because the threads look rougher and don't sit so beautifully after they have been washed. Others say you should, to remove the oils and acids transferred to your work from your hands while working the piece. Keep in mind that entries to needlework competitions are often required to be unwashed.

If you do decide to wash your work, use a gentle washing solution such as pure soap flakes. Handwash only, and immediately after washing lay your piece of work flat on a towel in the shade to dry. Do not wring or scrub the fabric! If you choose to wash your needlework, it should only be to remove oils and acids – if you treated it carefully when creating it, you should be able to avoid washing.

IRONING HARDANGER

When ironing a piece of finished Hardanger, always iron work from the back and place a thick fluffy towel between the worked piece and your ironing board. This will mean that the threads are not flattened too much, while still refreshing the fabric. For stubborn creases, cover the back of your work with a damp cloth and iron as described above.

CARING FOR FINISHED EMBROIDERY

Do not store needlework in plastic bags. The chemicals in the plastic may react with your work and destroy it. If plastic bags are necessary, only use acid-free, archival quality bags. An alternative would be to roll your work in acid-free tissue paper. If folding of the work for storage is necessary, periodically refold the work along different lines.

Treat all needlework with respect. As an embroiderer you will appreciate how much effort and time is invested in each piece. Make sure it will be around for future generations to enjoy also!

Stitch instructions

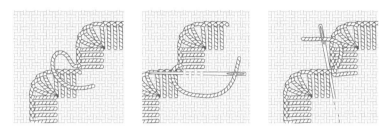

and techniques

Notes

The difficulty rating of each stitch or stitch combination is indicated by a cotton reel symbol next to the heading for each stitch.

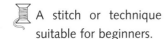 A stitch or technique suitable for beginners.

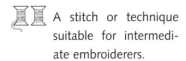 A stitch or technique suitable for intermediate embroiderers.

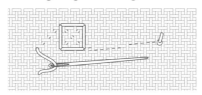 A stitch or technique suitable for advanced Hardanger embroiderers.

Stitches may have variations with differing levels of difficulty. In these cases, the difficulty rating is shown beside the heading for each variation. Fundamental techniques and information which are for all stitchers do not show a rating.

The stitch diagrams in this book use the following convention: the heavier weight threads are shown as striped, and the lighter weight threads are plain.

Practise each of the stitches before working on the projects. This will mean that by the time you come to do the projects you will feel much more confident with the stitches. You can use the sample pieces to build up a record of your stitching experience by assembling them in a scrapbook or folder.

Starting with a waste knot

A waste knot is used to secure a thread in an area where there is no previous stitching.

METHOD 1

1 Work out where the new stitching needs to begin and where the stitching line will continue. Tie a knot in the end of the thread, large enough not to slip through the holes in the fabric.

2 From the front of the fabric enter the needle about 10cm from where the stitching needs to begin. The waste knot should sit loosely on the front of the fabric. Make sure it is well away from any subsequent stitching. Begin stitching.

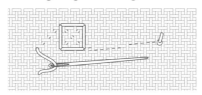

3 When a reasonable amount of stitching has been completed, cut off the knot and ease the end through to the back. Thread the needle onto this end and work it into the back of the stitching to secure it.

METHOD 2

❶ *This method works well when there is to be a long straight line of stitching.*

1 Work out where the new stitching needs to begin and where the stitching line will continue. Tie a knot in the end of the thread, large enough not to slip through the holes in the fabric.

2 From the front of the fabric enter the needle about 5 cm away from the beginning point, where it will be covered by the subsequent line of stitching. Bring the needle back through to the front at the beginning point of the stitching. The waste knot should sit loosely on the front of the fabric.

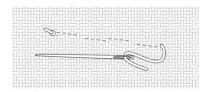

3 Begin stitching, checking that the waste knot thread is caught into the back of the stitches. When the stitching passes the waste knot, carefully cut off the knot without damaging any of the stitches. Ease the end of the thread through to the back of the fabric.

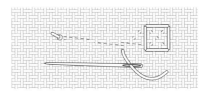

Starting a thread

1 Thread the needle with the new thread. With the back of the fabric facing you, take the thread through the back of about 5cm worth of stitches closest to where you need to continue stitching. If the previous thread was secured under the same threads to finish, make sure the new thread does not pull it back out again by holding its end as you begin the new one.

2 Give the thread a very light tug to check that it is reasonably secure. If not, work through the back of a few more stitches or take a small backstitch through the back of the stitches.

❶ *When working pulled thread stitches, make sure the new thread is well secured. Because of the tension needed to work the stitch, if the new thread is not well secured it will slip out again as you begin to stitch.*

❶ *If there is no previous stitching adjacent to where you need to stitch, use the waste knot method as described on page 17.*

Finishing a thread

To finish off a thread, work with the back of the fabric facing you. Slide the needle under the back of the last few stitches. With kloster blocks I usually take the thread through the back of at least five blocks. For other stitches take the needle through a similar distance.

❶ *Always make sure you leave enough thread to enable you to secure it well. If you don't have enough thread to end off, undo a few stitches to give you more length to work with.*

❶ *Never finish a thread halfway through a kloster block or any other stitch combination. Doing so can cause the stitch to sit wrongly, and could cause your stitch tension to go awry.*

If the thread you are using has become slightly worn, the new thread will look considerably different next to it, making the thread change very obvious. This effect will be lessened if the thread is changed at the end of a kloster block.

Stitching order

It is important to stitch Hardanger embroidery in the correct order. Because Hardanger often involves the cutting and removal of threads, eventually you pass the "point of no return". Much of the embroidery should be done before this point. Errors can easily be made and it is better to find and correct these before it is too late. Following the correct stitching order will assist in this.

❶ *Use the counted tacking to assist with positioning the first stitches correctly.*

HEM
If the design requires a hem, sew this first, following the project instructions.

KLOSTER BLOCKS AND SATIN STITCH
Always begin stitching the kloster blocks or satin stitch kloster block substitutes that are closest to the centre of the design, then work towards the outer edges.

Stitch the first kloster block and check again that it is in the correct place. Fix any mistakes and continue on. Regularly check that the kloster blocks line up with the counted tacking and opposite kloster blocks. When the ends of the rounds meet up with their beginning it will help to verify that counting mistakes have not been made.

BUTTONHOLE EDGING
After the kloster blocks, if there is a buttonhole edging, stitch it next. Do

not stitch the lacy buttonhole edge at this point – it will be completed with the needleweaving.

EYELETS
Next stitch any eyelets.

PULLED OR DRAWN THREAD WORK
Complete any pulled or drawn thread work, such as faggot stitch, or four-sided stitch.

NEEDLEWEAVING
Cut and remove the threads and complete the needleweaving (including any lacy buttonhole edge). This is the point of no return – if any elements are incorrectly placed, it will be extremely difficult to fix them successfully after the threads are cut.

SURFACE STITCHERY
Complete any surface stitchery such as satin stitch or cable stitch.

BEADING
Sew any beading.

CUT OUT
Lastly, cut the design from the surrounding fabric if required.

❶ *Always read through the instructions for each project before commencing. This will familiarise you with the process for that particular project.*

Kloster blocks

Kloster blocks are the basic building blocks of all Hardanger designs. They are made up of five satin stitches over a square of four threads. Kloster blocks are the first stitches worked in a Hardanger design, with the heavier of the two weights of cotton being used.

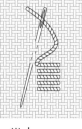

Kloster blocks are most commonly stitched in diagonal lines. Less commonly, they are stitched in line with the fabric's grain. When stitching kloster blocks it is important to count carefully. As they are the foundation for all other parts of Hardanger designs, care should be taken to make sure all elements are in the correct place from the outset.

DIAGONAL LINES
1 Bring the needle out from the back to the front of the fabric. Insert the needle four threads to the right. Bring the needle out again, one thread up from the beginning of the first stitch.

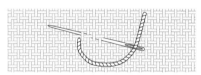

2 Continue, making each stitch one thread higher than the previous one, until there are five parallel stitches.

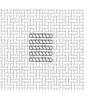

3 Bring the needle out again through the same hole as for the beginning of the last stitch. Count four threads up and enter the needle. Bring it out again one thread to the left of the base of the previous stitch.

4 Continue working left, with each stitch one thread to the left of the previous one until there are five parallel stitches. This completes the second kloster block.

5 To begin the third kloster block, count four stitches to the left of the end of the last stitch and bring the needle up as before. Repeat the instructions to build up a line of kloster blocks.

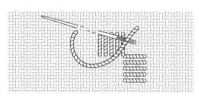

❶ *The back of the work should look like the line of stitching below left. If it looks like the line on the right, the direction has been reversed in error (two errors shown).*

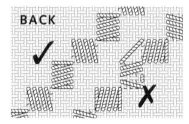

STRAIGHT LINES
Work the first kloster block. Leave a space of four threads and work another block. Continue in the same

way, building up a straight line of kloster blocks in which all blocks face the same direction.

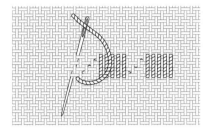

❶ The back of the work should look like the top line of stitching below. If it looks like the bottom line, the direction has been reversed in error (two errors shown).

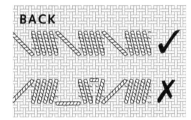

MISTAKES TO WATCH OUT FOR

It is very easy to make mistakes while stitching kloster blocks. As they are the first elements of the design to be stitched, there is often only the counted tacking to cross check against. As you stitch check, check and recheck that all your stitching is in the correct place!

❶ When stitching in diagonal lines the corners of kloster blocks touch.

❶ Make sure that the tension is constant throughout. Tension that is too tight will cause the fabric's threads to bunch up. Tension that is too loose will mean that the

threads are in danger of getting caught between the scissor blades when cutting the fabric's threads.

❶ Kloster blocks stretch over four threads in each direction. Both the examples below are incorrect.

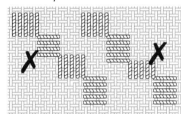

❶ For each kloster block the thread should spiral around the fabric's threads. Never bring the needle out of the hole next to the one that the needle just entered. When the fabric's threads are subsequently cut the stitches will unravel as they do not wrap around them. As you can see from the diagram, the stitches will also sit incorrectly.

❶ When stitching diagonal lines of kloster blocks, they should alternate horizontal, vertical, horizontal, vertical.

Satin stitch

The satin stitch used to make kloster blocks can also be used to create other shapes such as the stars and ships that are traditionally used in Hardanger. The chart symbols for satin stitch are parallel lines.

STARS

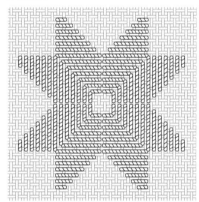

Stars can be of varying sizes. Follow the chart pattern for each star.

1 Each section of the star is worked as a group of stitches. Start with the stitches in the centre of the star 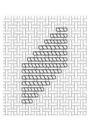 and work out to the edge of each section.

2 When you reach the outer edge, working from the back, take the thread in behind the 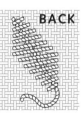 stitches back to the middle, ready to begin stitching the next section. Do not lace the thread across the back of the fabric to the next section.

SHIPS

Ships are so named because of their resemblance to Viking ships. These shapes are often worked in groups.

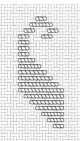

As for the petals of the star, work each one as a separate entity, at the end bringing the thread through the back of the stitches ready to begin the next one in the centre of the ship cluster.

OTHER SHAPES

Satin stitch can also be used to create various other shapes and groupings that are used as surface stitchery decoration or kloster block substitutes.

Eyelets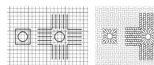

Eyelets are a pulled thread stitch worked over blocks of four by four threads. They create a small hole in the fabric and are often positioned in the centre of a kloster block cluster.

1 Bring the needle up in the corner of a block of four by four threads. Enter the needle in the centre of the block. Bring it back out again, one thread to the right of the first stitch.

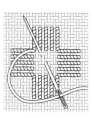

❶ *After each stitch give the thread a tug to tighten and to create the hole in the middle of the eyelet. Use even tension throughout to create a regular shaped hole.*

2 Enter the needle in the centre. Continuing in the same way, work along to the end of the four thread block, and then work down the next side.

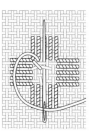

3 Complete the third side and the fourth side. There should be five stitches along each side of the eyelet.

❶ *Once the last stitch of the combination is complete, turn the fabric*

over. Take the needle under the thread which travelled from the previous eyelet to the beginning of the newly completed eyelet. This helps to tension the last stitch so that it does not show up as being obviously the last stitch.

BACK

❶ *When working eyelets in a row of kloster blocks, to travel between blocks, work the thread into the back of the kloster blocks. Do not lace the thread across the back of the fabric.*

❶ *When working a single eyelet in the middle of an expanse of fabric, catch the beginning of the thread in behind the stitches as you work. Once the eyelet is complete, use a fine sharp pointed needle such as a crewel needle to work the thread end into the back of the stitches. As the eyelet's stitches are tight, work slowly, taking the needle and thread under only one or two stitches at a time. Be careful not to pull the eyelet out of shape. When the thread is secure in the back of the eyelet, trim away any excess tail of thread.*

Cutting and removing threads for needleweaving

It is imperative to get this part of your embroidery right! If you make a mistake with the cutting of the threads it can be a very laborious task to correct it. Take your time, work carefully and only attempt the cutting of threads when your mind is clear and fresh.

When cutting threads it is important to make sure all kloster blocks and eyelets have been stitched beforehand. This is so that you are certain that all elements are in the correct position.

If you try to stitch an eyelet close to the cut thread ends, the eyelet will pull the fabric's threads and the fabric may fray; therefore they must be complete before any cutting is commenced.

When cutting the threads in the area to be needlewoven, remove only small sections of thread at a time and then stitch that section. If you remove too much, the fabric may lose its firmness and become unstable. The more stable the fabric remains, the easier it is to gain a good result.

WHERE TO CUT

Not all of the fabric threads are removed in needleweaving areas. A grid of threads is required as the foundation for weaving. Threads are grouped in fours, with alternate groups removed and remaining.

Each kloster block has two sides where the stitches begin or end, and two ends where the stitches stretch from side to side. Always cut on the sides, perpendicular to the direction of the stitches. The kloster block stitches will wrap around the uncut section of fabric, thereby effectively overcasting the edge to keep it from fraying. Never cut parallel to the stitches!

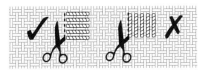

❷ *There is a right and a wrong way to use your scissors when cutting threads. Regardless of whether you are right- or left-handed, always keep the scissors on the left and the kloster block on the right. Scissors are made so that their blades will cut more closely if used this way.*

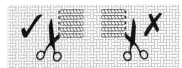

1 With the area to be removed on the left, and the kloster block on the right, carefully slip the blade of the scissors in behind the four threads you need to cut. (Do not cut yet!)

2 When the point of the blade has passed the fourth thread return it to the front of the fabric through the next hole in the fabric. Check that the threads are the four you need to cut.

3 Carefully snip the fabric threads as close as possible to the stitches, making sure that none are caught between the blades.

4 Work along the row of kloster blocks, taking care to cut only at the sides of the kloster blocks, not at the ends.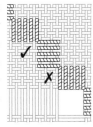

5 When both ends of the threads in the section to be removed have been cut, remove the threads one at a time. Trying to remove more than one will cause the threads to snag and bunch up.

❷ *Do not cut and withdraw all the threads that need to be removed at once. This will cause the fabric to destabilise. Only remove small sections of thread in the immediate vicinity of the needleweaving currently being worked. As you come to the edge of the removed sections, remove more and continue sewing.*

FIXING MISTAKES

If you make a mistake, all is not lost! If you have cut a thread in error carefully remove only the section that falls within the needleweaving area.

1 Remove one of the fabric's threads from along the edge of the

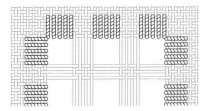

fabric piece. This will be used to replace the one cut in error. If your fabric is too small to allow you to remove a thread of useful length, choose a weight of pearl cotton that is similar in thickness to that of the fabric's threads.

2 Anchor the thread in the back of nearby kloster blocks. Start off by weaving under and over a few of the existing cross threads at the edge of the needleweaving area. Carefully weave the thread back into position, making sure that the tension is the same as that of the fabric's threads. Finish off by securing in the back of the kloster blocks.

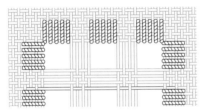

If you have mistakenly cut a whole group of four threads, replace using the method described for a single thread, weaving back and forth across the area to be replaced.

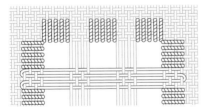

If you accidentally cut the threads on the wrong side of the kloster blocks, gently and carefully pull the threads, one at a time, across from the edge of the fabric. (Tweezers may be helpful.) Pull just enough across to thread a needle and then carefully weave the extra through the fabric underneath the kloster

block to overlap the threads that are already there. Try not to disturb the existing threads.

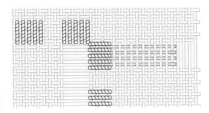

❶ *This will leave a gap at the edge of the fabric where the thread has been moved. If there is not enough spare fabric around the edge to allow for this, replace the thread with one taken from the side of the fabric, or matching pearl cotton.*

❶ *Every time the fabric structure is tampered with in any way, by the moving or replacing of threads, it weakens. Try to avoid making cutting mistakes!*

Needleweaving

Needleweaving forms an open mesh in the cutwork part of Hardanger. There are many different filling stitches, and most are based on a woven mesh of bars.

All needleweaving is stitched in the lighter or thinner of the two weights of thread.

Needleweaving often requires very careful planning for the stitching order. When working some of the advanced stitches it can be easy to end up in a corner with nowhere to go. Careful planning will help to avoid such difficulties.

Work the area to be needlewoven in a methodical order. Usually needleweaving is worked along straight lines, or as a zigzag. Some designs suit one method more than the other.

TO BEGIN NEEDLEWEAVING
1 To fasten the beginning of the thread, from the back of the fabric run it under the five kloster blocks

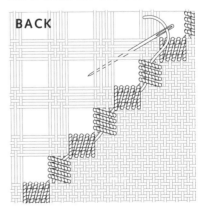

BACK

nearest to where you need to begin. The same principle is also used to secure the end of a thread to finish.

2 Take the needle through to the other side of the fabric in the centre of the bar to be woven. Turn the fabric over.

3 Take the needle around the two threads on the right and up through the centre of the bar again.

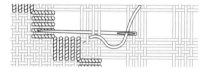

4 Take the needle around the two threads on the left and up through the centre.

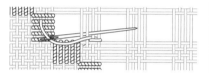

5 Repeat the steps, weaving around alternate sides until the bar is full.

❶ *Do not overwrap the bar. The stitches do not have to be crammed tightly together. There should be just enough to cover the whole bar, but no more. The number of stitches taken for each bar should remain constant over the whole Hardanger design. Make a note of the number of stitches for each bar on your pattern when you begin each project. Also make sure you keep the tension constant throughout.*

6 If the next bar to be woven follows in a straight line, finish the bar with the last stitch on the left (this will mean that there are an equal number of stitches on each side of the bar).

7 If the next bar to be woven is on the left, finish the bar with the last stitch on the right. Bring the thread under the woven square and up through the middle of the next bar to be woven.

8 If the next bar to be woven is on the right, finish the bar with the last stitch on the left.

❶ *It is important to make sure that the thread always ends the bar on the opposite side to the next bar which is to be stitched. This will correctly cause the thread to cross diagonally the back of the woven square of fabric. If the last stitch finishes on the same side as the next bar to be woven, the last stitch will not properly wrap the bar.*

Fancy needleweaving stitches such as picots and dove's eyes are worked as they are encountered. The mesh of the bars is woven at the same time as the fancy stitches; they are not added later.

WORKING STRAIGHT LINES
Needleweaving is often worked along lines of bars. It helps to keep the bars even and the fabric threads from moving around too much.

For a design worked on point (e.g. where the edges of the needleweaving are diagonal lines) when the stitching reaches the edge of the needleweaving area, turn 90 degrees and stitch the next line of bars.

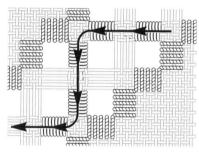

For a design not worked on point (e.g. a square), each subsequent line of needleweaving is parallel to the previous one. To travel to the next line, take the thread through the back of the adjacent kloster block.

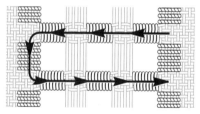

WORKING ZIGZAGS
Sometimes it may make more sense to work the needleweaving as a zigzag rather than in straight lines, (e.g. if the needleweaving section is worked on the diagonal and is long and narrow, with only one or two widths of needlewoven bars).

It is much easier to pull the mesh out of shape when zigzagging the needleweaving. Make sure you consistently weave the same number of times for each bar. This will help to avoid the mesh becoming uneven.

STARTING & FINISHING A THREAD IN THE MIDDLE OF NEEDLEWEAVING

Sometimes you may run out of thread in the middle of a section of needleweaving. When this happens there is no way of fastening the end of the thread behind the nearest kloster blocks.

It is very difficult to thread the new or old end in through the back of needleweaving as the tension is too tight to fit a needle through. This means that changing threads needs to be anticipated ahead of time. Get into the practice of anticipating how many more bars will be able to be completed with a thread nearing its end. This is a skill that will improve with practice. Until then, you may have to do a small amount of unpicking of stitches.

❶ *Never start or finish a thread in the middle of a woven bar. This will cause your tension to become sloppy or irregular. Always start or finish at the end of a bar, behind a woven square.*

1 To start a new thread, thread a second needle with the new thread. Make sure you have enough of the old thread left to complete two more bars and any fancy needleweaving that may be required in those two bars. If you don't have enough, unpick the needleweaving until you do.

2 Tie a small knot in the end of the new thread. From the front, take the needle with the new thread through the next woven square. Lace the thread along behind the next two bars (still unwoven at this

stage) and bring it out again in the centre of a woven square.

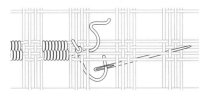

3 Changing back to the old thread, weave the next two bars, making sure that the new thread is caught into the back of the weaving. Take the needle behind the woven square and lace the thread behind the next two unwoven bars and bring it out through the next woven square.

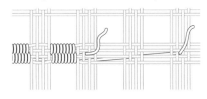

4 Return the end of the new thread to the back of the fabric through the hole it exited. Bring it out in the middle of the next bar.

5 Go back to the knot at the beginning of the new thread. Cut it off and ease the end through to the back of the fabric.

6 Continue needleweaving with the new thread, catching in the old thread on one side of the weaving at the back for the next two bars. When you have passed where the old thread comes out through the woven square, carefully cut off the remains of the old thread and ease the end through to the back of the fabric.

BACKING OUT OF A CORNER

Occasionally you may find the stitching has come to a dead end, with nowhere to end the thread.

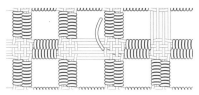

1 Undo the stitching to a point where you are able to keep going in another direction (the beginning of the dead end).

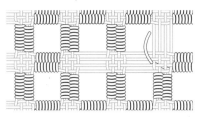

2 From the back, lace the thread to the far end of the dead end. Catch the thread in behind one fabric thread in each woven square that is passed. Fasten the thread at the end of the dead end by catching it in behind a stitch or thread.

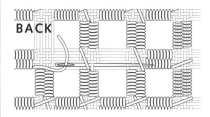

3 Take the thread through to the front in the centre of the bar at the end and begin needleweaving back in the other direction.

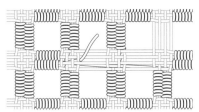

LACING THREAD ACROSS THE BACK

When difficult combination stitches that take up more than one row are stitched in the middle of needle-weaving, it often helps to leave a space for them so that they can be worked later in one go. This is a variation of the technique for lacing when working a dead end.

1 The rows on the perimeter of the stitch are worked as usual.

❶ *When the combination involves stitches which are worked through the bars along the perimeter of the stitch combination (e.g. triangular webs, twisted Ys), it is necessary for the edge rows to be worked first. Otherwise there will not be anywhere to properly anchor the stitch.*

2 At the position for the stitch com-bination, instead of weaving the next bar, lace the thread behind the 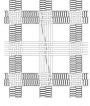 next two bars, and bring it out in the third bar. Weave the third bar as normal.

3 For the centre row in the other direction, lace the thread behind the next two bars, and 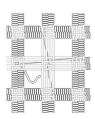 secure it behind the next woven square, or by taking a small stitch over one of the threads. Bring the thread out in the space, ready to work the stitch com-bination.

4 Sew the stitch combination and continue on by weaving the next bar.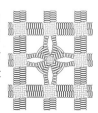

Wrapped bars

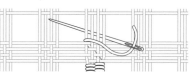

As an alternative to weaving bars together, they can be wrapped. Wrapped bars are frequently used as part of some of the more difficult needleweaving stitch combinations. They can be worked over two threads or four.

❶ *Wrapped bars are generally not satisfactory as a needleweaving filling stitch as they can very easily pull out of shape and become uneven. In the projects in this book they are only used as elements in combination stitches.*

1 Bring the needle out beside the threads to be wrapped. Take the needle over the fabric threads and down on the other side. Bring it out again next to where the needle first came up.

2 Repeat wraps until the bar is filled. The threads should sit next to each other and not overlap. Do not wrap the bars too full as they may buckle or bow.

❶ *If you must work wrapped bars as a filling stitch, always work them in straight lines rather than as zigzags. This will help to keep them even.*

Dove's eye stitch

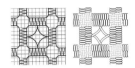

Dove's eye stitch is a diamond shaped needleweaving stitch, frequently used for filling large areas of needleweaving.

1 Dove's eye stitch is worked during the fourth side of a square of needleweaving. The other three sides should already have been worked so that the stitch can be anchored into woven bars. Weave halfway along the fourth bar. Loop the thread across to the centre of the adjacent bar. Enter the bar from behind, and bring out to the front.

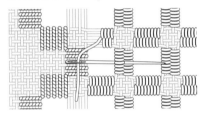

2 Take the needle behind the looped stitch. Enter the centre of the next bar from behind and bring the needle out.

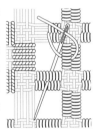

3 Repeat for the next bar.

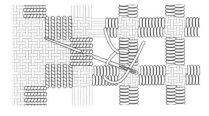

❶ *When kloster blocks form one or more of the sides to the square*

where the dove's eye is to be worked, the thread should split the centre stitch of the kloster block.

4 Take the needle over the first looped stitch, under the two nearest fabric threads of the bar and out through the centre of the bar. Continue weaving to finish the bar.

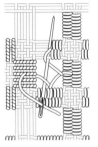

❶ *All dove's eyes need to twist the same way. All the sides of the dove's eye must be the same length or the stitch will look uneven. The same tension should be used throughout the embroidery so that the central diamond is the same size from stitch to stitch.*

DOVE'S EYE IN A WRAPPED CIRCLE

When stitching this combination, work the wrapped circle first and then the dove's eye.

1 Bring the needle up through the centre of the first unwoven bar, and wrap the outer two threads on the right. Wrap tightly, overfilling

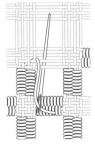

slightly so that the bar bows outwards. Do not allow the threads to overlap.

2 Wrap the outer bars on the other three sides in the same way, to create the circle.

3 Bring the needle out in the centre. Wrap three inner bars. Do not overwrap.

4 To complete the stitch combination, wrap the fourth side, incorporating a dove's eye stitch.

Four-sided stitch

Four-sided stitch is a pulled thread stitch commonly used in Hardanger. It can be pulled tight to make lacy holes in the fabric (see bottom right), or stitched with regular tension as a surface stitch, to create a line of boxes.

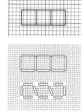

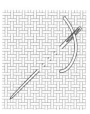

1 Bring the needle out and count up four threads. Enter the needle into the fabric. Count down four threads and four to the left and bring the needle out again. The thread exits the fabric four threads to the left of the bottom of the first stitch.

❶ *To use four-sided stitch as a pulled thread stitch, pull each of the stitches to tighten it as you work it. To work as a surface stitch only, work with regular tension.*

2 Enter the needle at the bottom of the first stitch (four threads to the right of where the needle exited

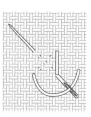

last). Bring the needle out of the fabric four threads up and four to the left. The thread will now exit the fabric four threads to the left of the top of the first stitch. On the back, the stitches form a cross.

3 Enter the needle four threads to the right, at the top of the first stitch. Bring the needle out of the

fabric in the opposite corner of the square. The back of the stitches still forms a cross, but one of the cross pieces is double.

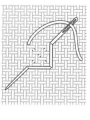

4 To complete the first stitch combination and begin the second one, take the needle up four threads and enter. Count four threads down and four to the left and take the needle back through to the front of the fabric.

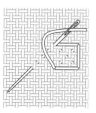

5 Continue working through each of the steps to create a line of four-sided stitch.

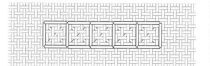

Cable stitch

Cable stitch is a surface stitch useful for creating texture and lines. It can be worked as a single row or as two adjacent rows (double cable stitch).

1 Bring the needle out of the fabric. Enter it again diagonally two threads above and two to the right. Bring the needle out two threads to the left (two threads above the beginning of the first stitch).

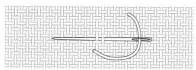

2 Enter the needle two threads above the top of the last stitch. Bring it out again through the same hole as the end of the last stitch.

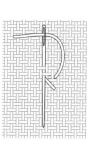

❶ *The needle lies parallel to the fabric's threads. The stitches are diagonal across the fabric.*

3 Repeat the steps to build up a line of cable stitch.

For double cable stitch, work an adjacent row of cable stitch, with one side of the row entering the same holes as for the first.

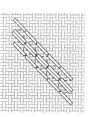

Algerian eyelet stitch

Algerian eyelets are usually worked as a surface stitch, but by tightening the tension, they can be used as a pulled thread stitch. Similar to eyelets, Algerian eyelets are worked over a block of four by four threads, but have only three stitches in each side, as opposed to the five for eyelet stitch.

SINGLE STITCHES

1 Bring the needle up in the corner of a block of four by four threads. Enter the needle through the centre of the 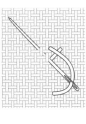 block of threads (two stitches down, two across). Bring the needle out again two stitches to the left of where the needle first exited, and two above where the needle entered.

2 Enter the needle through the centre and bring it out again in the next corner of the block of four by four threads.

3 Continue, bringing the needle out of every second hole around the edge of the block until the eyelet is complete.

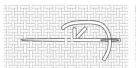

AS A DIAGONAL ROW

The stitching is done in two stages: a journey to the end of the row, and a journey back again. Half of each stitch combination is worked along the line of eyelets for the first journey. On the return journey the other half of each stitch is worked, thus completing the line of eyelets.

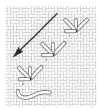 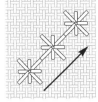

Beading

1 To attach beads, use No.12 pearl cotton or one strand of stranded embroidery cotton in a colour that matches the beads. Thread onto a beading needle.

2 Secure the thread in the back of some nearby stitches. Bring the needle out through the hole where the bead is required.

3 Thread a bead onto the needle and thread. Take the needle back through the same hole in the fabric that the thread came out of.

4 Repeat instructions for subsequent beads.

❶ *To move to the next bead's position, from the back of the fabric take the thread through the back of any stitching which lies in between. If there is no stitching in between, lace the thread across the back of the fabric. The thread should not be too tight or too loose, but should lie flat against the fabric.*

Buttonhole edge

Buttonhole edge forms a firm edge, allowing the surrounding material to be cut from it to create unusual shapes. It is often used in conjunction with an inner row of kloster blocks. If eyelets are used, they provide extra strength. Although the edge is reasonably stable, care should be taken with its handling and laundering.

1 Bring the needle and thread out of the fabric. Enter the needle point four threads down and one to the left. Bring the needle point back out in the hole to the left of where the needle first exited the fabric.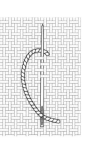

2 Wrap the thread behind the needle point and pull the needle and thread through. Repeat for each stitch as needed.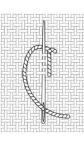

❶ *It is easier to work buttonhole stitch with a sewing motion (as illustrated in the diagrams, where the needle goes in the fabric and out again in one movement) than a stabbing motion (taking the needle and thread through to the back of the fabric, and then in another movement, returning to the front).*

TURNING AN OUTSIDE CORNER

1 When an outside corner is reached, enter the needle point in the same hole as for the last stitch on 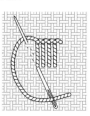 the straight section. Bring the point out again two threads to the left of the top of the previous stitch. Wrap the thread behind the needle point. Pull the needle and thread through.

2 Enter the needle point through the same hole as the bottom of the previous stitch. Exit the needle 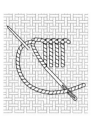 point one thread to the left and one down from the top of the last stitch. Wrap the thread behind the point and pull the needle and thread through.

3 Enter the needle point through the same hole as the bottom of the previous stitch. Exit the needle point one thread to the left and one down from the top of the last stitch. Wrap the thread behind the point and pull the needle and thread through.

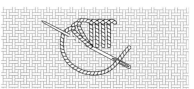

4 Enter the needle point through the same hole as the bottom of the previous stitch. Exit the needle point two threads below the top of the last stitch. Wrap the thread behind

the point and pull the needle and thread through. Continue on stitching buttonhole in a straight line.

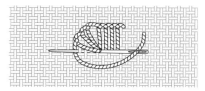

❶ *Do not overtighten the stitches as you turn the corner. Doing so will cause the corner pivoting hole to become enlarged, forming a large gap in the fabric.*

TURNING AN INSIDE CORNER

Complete the last stitch before turning the corner. Enter the needle four threads below the loop end of the previous stitch. 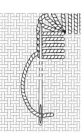 Bring the needle point out of the same hole as for the loop end of the previous stitch. Bring the point up over the top of the loop. Wrap the thread around the needle point and pull the needle through. Continue stitching as required by the pattern.

JOINING THE END TO THE BEGINNING

Typically the beginning of a buttonhole edge will be on a straight section of sewing, or on an inside corner. When the sewing has been completed for the whole round, the end needs to slip into the beginning to form an invisible join.

For an inside corner

1 Finish the last stitch to complete the round.

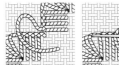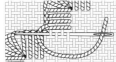

2 Take the needle under the top loop of the very first stitch in the buttonhole edge. Enter the needle into the fabric

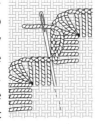

from the front, through the hole to the right of the bottom of the first stitch. Pull the needle through and secure the thread end into the back of the stitches.

❶ *The last stitch does not double up with the first stitch. It fits into the stitch sequence and makes the beginning and end invisible.*

For a straight section

Complete the last stitch to finish the round. Take the needle in under the loop of the very first stitch of the buttonhole edge. Enter the needle into the fabric from the

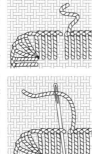

front, through the hole to the right of the bottom of the first stitch. Pull the needle through and secure the thread end into the back of stitches.

❶ *The last stitch does not double up with the first stitch. It fits into the stitch sequence and makes the beginning and end invisible.*

CUTTING FROM THE FABRIC

When cutting a buttonhole edge from the surrounding fabric, work slowly and with great care. As it is the final step, it would be a great pity to make a mistake!

❶ *Always work from the back. If you work from the front you will not be able to see where to cut because the looped edge will obscure your view. Whether you are right- or left-handed, you should work with the embroidery on the right and the scissors on the left. Scissors are designed to cut more closely when positioned this way.*

1 Slip the scissors point under a group of four threads. Manoeuvre it as you slide it in so that it will

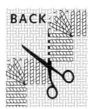

cut as close as possible to the stitching, without catching any of the embroidery threads. If you are unsure whether any have been caught in, turn the work over to check from the front as well as the back. When you are satisfied that all is well, return the point of the scissors to the surface through the last hole and carefully snip through the four threads.

2 When cutting an outside corner, the threads need to be cut individually or in pairs of threads that cross

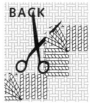

over. Work slowly, slipping the point of the scissors carefully underneath a single thread or a pair of threads.

Check that no embroidery threads are caught. Return the point to the surface and carefully snip the threads.

❶ *Work slowly! It is very tempting to rush this final stage. Don't take the chance of spoiling all the hard work you have put in by making a difficult to repair mistake at this point.*

MISTAKES WHILE CUTTING

As the fabric has been cut away, it is more difficult to repair this sort of mistake.

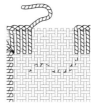

1 Carefully undo the stitching on either side of the cut so that you have just enough thread to secure it into the back of the work. Take care to disturb the fabric threads as little as possible. Be particularly careful around corners as the fabric can very easily fray.

2 Secure the ends. Use a fresh piece of thread to re-stitch the removed section. Because there are no fabric holes to stitch

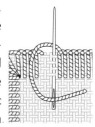

through on the outer edge where the fabric has been cut away, copy the tension used for the surrounding stitching to make the edge look as similar as possible.

3 Thread the last stitch carefully through the first

stitch to create an invisible join.

Spider's web

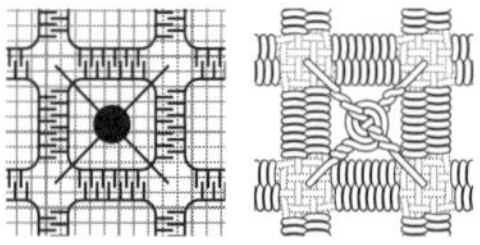

Spider's webs are a needleweaving filling stitch.

1 Needleweave or sew three of the sides of the square. (In the diagram, right, two sides are kloster blocks.) Bring the needle and thread out of the centre of the adjacent woven square of fabric in the needleweaving foundation mesh. Take it diagonally across to the opposite corner of the open square, entering the centre of the woven square from beneath the fabric. Bring the needle and thread through to the front of the fabric.

2 With the needle point towards the unwoven bar, pass it under the diagonal thread and wind it around three or four times. Do not overcrowd the twisting. Give the needle and thread a small tug to intertwine the two threads. Bring the needle up through the centre of the unwoven bar.

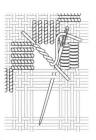

3 Needleweave the fourth side of the square. Bring the needle out of the centre of the adjacent woven

square. To make the second diagonal, take the needle over the first diagonal twist. Enter the needle from the back of the fabric, in the centre of the opposite corner's woven square.

4 Twist the thread once or twice around the first half of the second diagonal thread. Take the thread under the diagonal cross, bringing the needle out on the other side.

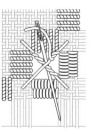

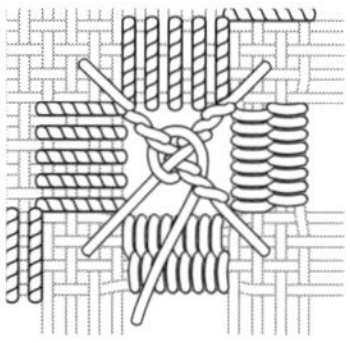

5 Circling around the spokes of the web, pass the needle over the top of the untwisted section of the second diagonal. Take it under the next spoke, over the next and under the next. This will complete the first circle. Give the thread a small tug to tighten it around the spokes.

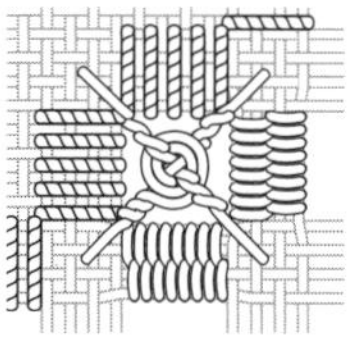

6 Continue to weave the thread around the spokes until the web is the desired size. Finish the web by winding the thread around the untwisted section of the second diagonal. Give the thread a small tug to intertwine all the threads and secure the end at the back of the fabric.

❷ *The threads in the circular part of the web should sit next to each other. They should not be so tight*

as to overlap or pull the centre out of shape. Equally the threads should not be too loose either. Make a note of how many times the thread circles the web so that you can be consistent throughout.

❶ *All the diagonals should cross the same way. To do this, depending on which axis the first diagonal is on, the second one should either go over the top or underneath it. Choose which axis will be the top axis and work all other webs accordingly.*

Faggot stitch

Faggot stitch is a pulled thread stitch which creates a firm open mesh. As it is worked on the diagonal, care needs to be taken so that the fabric is not pulled out of shape. Best results are achieved when using cotton that is the same colour as the fabric.

1 Bring the needle out of the fabric. Count two threads to the right. Enter the needle and bring it out again through the first hole.

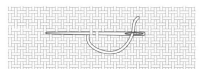

2 Take the needle back to the second hole; enter the needle. Count two threads left and two up, and bring the needle back out again.

3 Enter the needle in the first hole, count two threads up and exit from the same hole as for the last stitch.

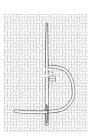

4 Enter the needle into the same hole as for the previous stitch. Count two threads up and left and bring the needle out again.

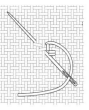

5 Work through the instructions, repeating as needed.

❶ *Each bar of the mesh is made by two stitches. On the back of the work, diagonal stitches are used to move to the next bar.*

❶ *Additional rows are worked adjacent to the first row.*

Greek cross

The Greek cross is a very versatile stitch. It can be used as a single combination, in a row, or in reverse. Greek crosses can also be used in conjunction with other stitches to create fancy stitch combinations. Each version uses the same principles to create the stitch but with quite different effects.

QUARTER CROSS FOUNDATION STITCH

The quarter cross forms the foundation of all the Greek cross stitches.

1 Bring the needle out of the fabric to the left of an unwoven bar. Wrap the thread around two fabric threads until you reach the middle.

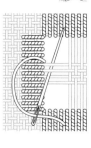

❶ *Do not overwrap. The wraps should lie next to each other on the bar and not overlap.*

2 Take the needle under the woven centre square of fabric. Bring it out in the centre of the adjacent bar which will next be wrapped.

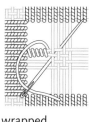

3 Take the thread around the left two threads of the adjacent unfilled bar and then back under the bar that has already been wrapped.

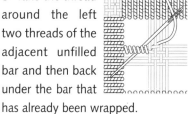

4 Continue to weave back and forth between the wrapped bar and the two threads of the next bar. Weave until half the distance along the bars is covered.

5 Wrap the empty section of the bar to complete the stitch sequence.

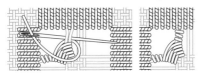

GREEK CROSS

1 Begin by working a quarter cross. Take the thread through to the back of the fabric and anchor close by in the back of the satin stitches or kloster blocks.

2 Work another quarter cross adjacent to the first.

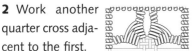

3 Continue with the quarter crosses until the Greek cross is complete.

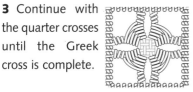

GREEK CROSS BORDER

1 Each set of four threads in the needleweaving area is divided into two sets of two. One set is used for the first line of stitching going one direction, and the other is for the second line of stitching going the other direction. Begin at A, working a quarter cross. Continue along the row of threads, working quarter crosses to fill the space available.

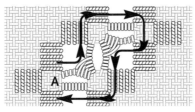

2 To turn the corner, work a single wrapped bar.

3 Work back along the second row, filling in the vacant threads with quarter crosses.

4 Finish with a single wrapped bar.

TURNING CORNERS

The instructions for corners in the outer row and the inner row are different.

The outer row

(Shown here as grey stitching.) When the outside corner is reached, wrap a single bar. Continue with a quarter cross for the next unwrapped bars.

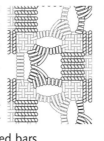

The inner row

(Shown here as grey stitching.) Complete a quarter cross on the first two of the

three unwrapped bars. At the third bar, complete another quarter cross over it and the previous bar. In this way, the two quarter crosses are combined. Continue with a quarter cross on the next unwrapped bars.

REVERSE GREEK CROSS

1 Begin by wrapping the outer two bars of each set.

2 Work a quarter cross on the first two bars.

3 Work a quarter cross on the second and third bar, overlapping the first one.

4 Work a third quarter cross in the next corner, overlapping the previous one. Work a fourth quarter cross on the last corner, finishing with the weaving stage. There will be no room left to wrap the final section of the bar, as it will already be covered by the first quarter cross. Slip the needle into the back of the first quarter cross and take the thread out to the edge of the needleweaving area to secure it.

Lacy buttonhole edge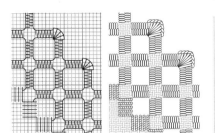

While this style of edge is very beautiful, it is reasonably unstable and therefore requires extra strengthening before stitching.

REMOVING THE THREADS

For the edge illustrated above, three rows need to be woven. Four rows of threads will need to be withdrawn to allow for the buttonhole corners. At the outer edge of the needleweaving area, cut the threads to be removed, so that the area beyond remains as fully woven fabric.

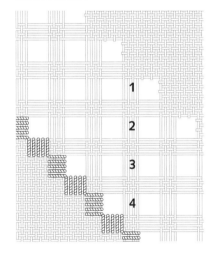

❶ *Do not remove too large a section of threads at once as this will cause the fabric to destabilise.*

LACING THE BACK

To ensure that the lacy buttonhole edge does not fall apart, you will need to lace a web of threads across the back of the outer two rows of the lacy edge. Use pearl cotton that is a similar thickness to the fabric's threads. The colour should also match the fabric. If an appropriate weight or colour is unavailable, remove a thread from the side of the fabric.

1 With the back of the work facing you, fasten a long thread of the lighter weight cotton in the back of kloster blocks nearest to the edge.

2 Lace the thread across the back, zigzagging over the two outer rows of the needleweaving area, taking a small backstitch at the corners.

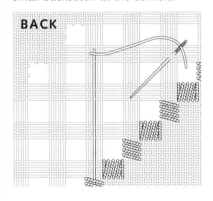

3 Build up a network of two rows of strengthening threads around the edge of the needleweaving area.

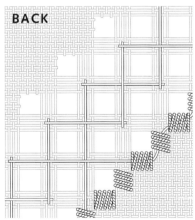

❶ *To start or finish a thread, secure it in the nearest kloster blocks.*

❶ *The threads should lie taut on the back of the fabric, but not so tight that they pucker the fabric. Regularly lay your work on a flat surface to check the tension.*

STITCHING THE EDGE

1 Weave the bars using the straight lines method, taking care to catch in the strengthening threads as you 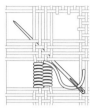 sew. When you reach an outer corner, take the thread behind the fabric to the opposite corner of the woven square.

2 Working back towards the woven bars, buttonhole the two outer edges of the woven square, pivoting in the inner corner. To finish the corner take the thread behind the fabric, through the back of the buttonhole stitches to the middle of the next bar, ready to begin weaving.

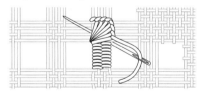

❶ *Around the outer edge of the corner there should be a stitch in between each of the fabric's threads. Do not miss working in any holes, unlike the regular buttonhole edge.*

❶ *Always stitch the buttonhole*
corner back towards the
previously woven bar. The corner
is not as strong if the buttonhole
is stitched in the same direction
as the needleweaving.

3 Continue weaving bars and
buttonholing corners as appropriate, according to the pattern.

STRAIGHT SIDES

When stitching a lacy buttonhole
edge along a straight side, you will
need to carefully plan your stitching
order according to the shape of the
edge. Draw a diagram and work out
the order before you begin stitching. The buttonhole corners should
be stitched as they are encountered.

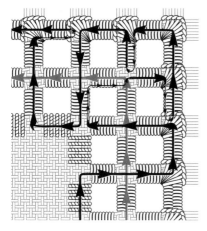

In the diagram above, the arrow
lines show the stitching order. The
grey arrow line is the second line
of stitching. The small black arrow
sections are laced along the back.

❶ *Never work the buttonhole edge*
as a single line of stitching.
Always zigzag back and forth
across the needleweaving area,
as this will give extra strength
to the edge.

CUTTING OUT

To cut the Hardanger from the
surrounding fabric, follow the
instructions 'Cutting from the fabric'
on page 31.

Knotted picot

Many Hardanger
embroiderers find picots
difficult. However, with
patience and persistence
they should be as easy as other
advanced stitches. There are many
ways of constructing a picot.
Two are shown in this book:
the knotted and the looped picot.
Picots can be worked on either
side of a bar or on just a
single side.

PICOT ON THE RIGHT

1 Begin by weaving halfway along
the bar (unless a picot has already
been completed on the left side, as
you will already be in the middle of
the bar), with the last stitch being
on the left-hand side of the bar. The
thread should exit the fabric in the
centre of the bar.

2 From the centre of the bar, enter
the needle point under the two
fabric threads on the right. Taking
the thread across the front of the
needle, wind the thread around the
point three times. Pull the needle
through and gradually tighten to
create a neat, firm knot.

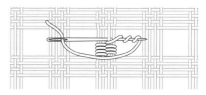

❶ *Make sure that the knot is firm*
before moving on to step 3.
Failure to do so could mean the
knot becomes untidy.

3 From the side, enter the needle
back underneath the two threads on
the right, and bring it out again

through the middle of the bar. This completes the first picot.

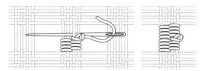

4 Continue weaving to the end of the bar, or complete a picot on the left side of the bar.

PICOT ON THE LEFT

1 Begin by weaving halfway along unless a picot has already been completed on the right. The last stitch should be on the right-hand side of the bar.

2 From the centre of the bar, enter the needle point under the two fabric threads on the left. Taking the thread across the front of the needle, wind the thread around the point three times. Pull the needle through and gradually tighten to create a neat, firm knot.

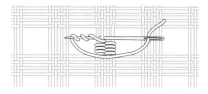

❶ *Make sure that the knot is firm before moving on to step 3. Failure to do so could mean the knot becomes untidy.*

3 From the side, enter the needle under the two threads on the left, with the needle coming out in the centre of the bar. This completes the picot.

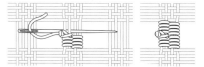

4 Continue weaving to the end of the bar, or create another picot on the right side of the bar.

PICOT ON THE SECOND SIDE

Before weaving to complete the bar, a second picot can be created opposite the first.

Enter the needle point under the two threads on the opposite side of the bar. Continue as for step 2 of the left- or right-sided picots.

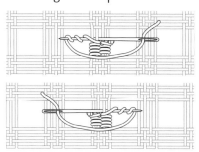

❶ *Practise picots on some scrap material until you are happy with your results because picots can be difficult to undo.*

Looped picot

Looped picots are a beautiful stitch which can be difficult to master. Practise until you have perfected the stitch because the results are worth it!

PICOT ON THE RIGHT

1 Weave half the bar, finishing with the last stitch on the left. Enter the needle point under the two fabric threads on the right.

2 Wind the thread behind the point of the needle, and around once more (one and a half times in total), finishing with the thread on the left of the needle point.

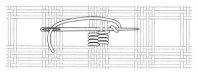

3 To make a very loose knot, gently tighten the thread by pulling the thread to the right.

4 Place the point of the needle into the loose knot, to the left of the first part of the thread.

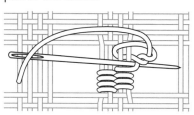

5 Gently pull the end of the thread. As it tightens, it should create a loop around the needle with a knot

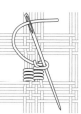

at its base. You may need to manipulate it a little for this to happen. Remove the needle point.

6 Place the point of a second needle in the loop. Take the thread behind the needle point and loop, from right to left.

7 Take the thread through the centre of the bar from the back to the front. Tug on the thread to firm the knot. Use the second needle point to tug in the opposite direction, to make sure that the loop stays upright and doesn't get pulled sideways. Remove the second needle.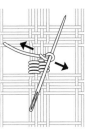

8 Continue to needleweave to the end of the bar or create another picot on the other side of the bar.

PICOT ON THE LEFT

1 Weave half the bar, finishing with the last stitch on the right. Enter the needle point under the two fabric threads on the left.

2 Wind the thread behind the point of the needle, and around once more (one and a half times in total), finishing with the thread on the right of the needle point.

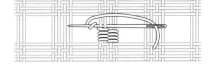

3 To make a very loose knot, gently tighten by pulling the thread to the left.

4 Place the point of the needle into the loose knot, to the right of the first part of the thread.

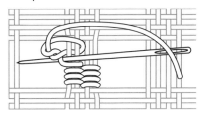

5 Gently pull the end of the thread. As it tightens, it should create a loop around the needle with a knot at its base. You  may need to manipulate it a little for this to happen. Remove the needle point.

6 Place the point of a second needle in the loop. Take the thread behind the needle point and loop, from left to right.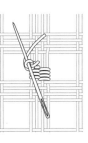

7 Take the thread through the centre of the bar from the back to the front. Tug on the thread to create a firm knot. Use the 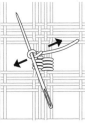 second needle point to tug in the opposite direction, to make sure that the loop stays upright and doesn't get pulled sideways. Remove the second needle.

8 Continue needleweaving to the end of the bar or create another picot on the other side of the bar.

PICOT ON THE SECOND SIDE

Before weaving to complete the bar, a second picot can be created opposite the first.

Enter the needle point under the two threads on the opposite side of the bar. Continue as for step 2 of either the left- or right-sided picots.

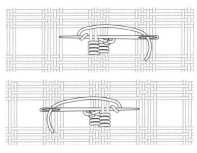

❶ *Practise picots on some scrap material until you are happy with your results because picots can be difficult to undo.*

Triangular webs with buttonhole bars

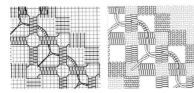

This stitch combination is worked as two separate lines: one line of buttonhole bars and one of twisted triangles.

BUTTONHOLE BARS

1 Weave one bar and half of the adjacent bar.

2 Loop the thread across to the first bar, entering the needle from the back into the centre of the bar.

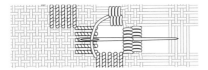

3 Loop back across to the second bar and enter from the back. Loop back to the first bar again.

❶ *Make sure the loops are not too loose or too tight. The right tension will come with practice.*

4 Buttonhole to cover the loops, travelling back towards the second bar. Do not overfill the bar.

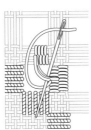

5 Enter the needle and thread into the back of the second bar, and then weave the remainder of the bar.

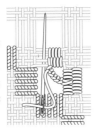

6 Repeat the steps along the row to fill the desired area.

TRIANGULAR WEBS

1 Bring the needle out in the centre of the woven square and enter it into the one of the bars on the opposite side of the open space. Take the needle point over the first loop of the triangular web. Pull the needle and thread through.

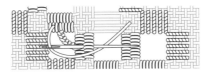

2 Take the needle through the centre of the adjacent woven bar, entering from the back. Take the needle under the second loop of the web, over the first and through to the back of the fabric.

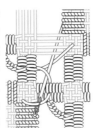

3 Turn the fabric over and bring the needle out. Secure the thread through the back of the initial thread leading to the web.

4 Weave two bars and repeat instructions to fill the desired space.

Twisted Y with looped picots

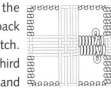

This combination stitch can be worked within an area of needleweaving or by itself.

1 Anchor the thread in the back of the satin stitch. Weave one third of the first bar and work a looped picot on either side of the bar. Weave to fill the remainder of the bar.

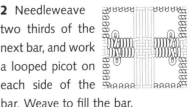

❶ *The picots should not sit in the middle of the bar; they should sit two thirds of the way along the bars, towards the outer ends.*

2 Needleweave two thirds of the next bar, and work a looped picot on each side of the bar. Weave to fill the bar.

3 Anchor the thread in the back of the surrounding satin stitch, and bring the needle out ready for the next bar.

4 Needleweave one third of the bar and work a looped picot on either side of the bar. Weave to fill the rest of the bar.

5 Bring the needle and thread out through the centre of the woven square in the middle of the needleweaving area. Enter the needle through the front of the middle of the left kloster block (as shown in diagram) or needlewoven bar.

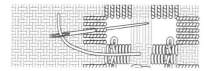

6 Take the thread over the first loop, around the back and over again. Enter the needle in the middle of the other kloster block from the front.

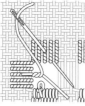

7 Take the thread over the second loop, around the back, and over again. Take the thread under the untwisted section of the first loop, around and over again. Enter the needle under the centre corner and secure at the back of the woven square.

8 Work a twisted Y in the other open squares. For the final unwoven bar, weave two thirds, work a looped picot on either side, and weave to fill the bar.

❶ *To work this combination within an area of needleweaving, always make sure the bars along the edges have been woven first. Otherwise there would be no weaving to anchor the webs into. You may need to carefully plan the stitching order and lace the thread across the back of some unwoven bars to do this.*

Spider's web in eyelets

This stitch can be adapted for fillings other than the spider's web. Dove's eyes and picots could also be used.

❶ *For this stitch combination, instead of leaving the four threads in the centre uncut, the four threads in the centre are removed, leaving the outer threads intact.*

1 Secure the end of the thread in the back of the adjacent satin stitch. Bring the needle out in a corner of the open square.

2 Work an eyelet in the woven square, catching in the thread that laced from the satin stitch to the beginning position, at the back of the fabric.

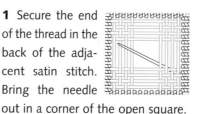

3 Weave the next bar. Bring the thread out in the corner of the open square.

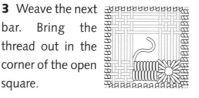

4 Work an eyelet in the woven square then weave the next bar.

5 From the centre of the adjacent woven square, take the first diagonal thread for the

spider's web across to the opposite corner. Twist the threads together on the return.

6 Work an eyelet in the woven corner, working either side of the diagonal. Weave the next bar.

7 Exit the thread through the centre of the next woven square. Work the remainder of the spider's web according to the instructions on page 32.

8 Work an eyelet in the final woven corner, working either side of the diagonal. Weave the next bar. Take the thread across the back to the nearest satin stitch and secure.

Hardanger projects

Patchwork cushion

This cushion beautifully combines patchwork and Hardanger. The outer Hardanger designs feature surface stitchery and are highlighted in green to match the patchwork. The centre design features elegant cream on cream.

DIFFICULTY Beginner
FINISHED SIZE 40 cm x 40 cm

See page 56 for a coloured photograph of this project.

MATERIALS
- 5 pieces 11 cm x 11 cm cream Hardanger fabric, 22 count
- 4 pieces 11 cm x 11 cm cream cotton fabric
- 75 cm patterned cotton fabric in green floral (120 cm wide approx.)
- 15 cm patterned cotton fabric in pink floral (120 cm wide approx.)
- 10 cm medium-weight fusible interfacing (full fabric width)
- 3.6 m cotton edging lace
- 2 x 18 mm buttons
- 35 cm cushion insert
- machine sewing threads to match green fabric and lace
- 1 skein No.5 DMC pearl cotton, colour 712 (cream)
- 1 skein No.5 DMC pearl cotton, to match green fabric
- 1 ball No.8 DMC pearl cotton, colour 712 (cream)
- No. 24 tapestry needle

STITCHES USED
Kloster blocks, satin stitch, eyelets, needleweaving bars, four-sided stitch, Algerian eyelet stitch.

EMBROIDERY

❶ *You must be accurate when positioning the embroidery in the centre of each patch.*

Design A
Work satin stitch ships in green pearl cotton. Stitch kloster blocks in corners with No. 5 pearl cotton, colour 712. Work eyelets in No. 8 pearl cotton, colour 712.

Design B
Work the satin stitch star in green pearl cotton. Sew eyelets and four-sided stitch with No. 8 pearl cotton, colour 712. The four-sided stitch should be worked as a surface stitch with regular tension.

Design C
Work kloster blocks in green pearl cotton. Sew eyelets, four-sided stitch (as a surface stitch), and all half Algerian eyelets in No. 8 pearl cotton, colour 712.

Design D
Work kloster blocks and ships in green pearl cotton. Work eyelets and four-sided stitch (as a surface stitch) in No.8 pearl cotton, colour 712.

Design E
Work all satin stitch in No. 5 pearl cotton, colour 712. Work Algerian eyelets in No. 8 pearl cotton, colour 712. Stitch needleweaving in No. 8 pearl cotton, colour 712.

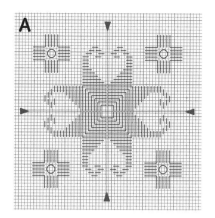

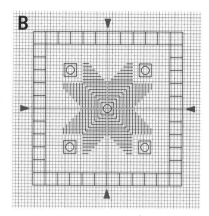

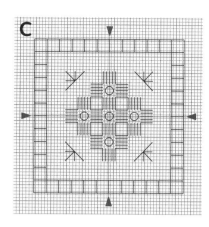

CONSTRUCTION

❗ *All seam allowances of 1.5cm are included in pattern pieces.*

1 Following the cutting layout shown below, from the green fabric cut:

    A: 2 pieces 7 cm x 35 cm

    B: 2 pieces 23.5 cm x 35 cm

    C: 2 pieces 11 cm x 11 cm

    D: 3 pieces 15 cm x full
        fabric width

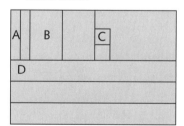

2 From the fusible interfacing cut:
2 pieces 4 cm x 35 cm.

3 Following the cutting layout shown below, from the pink fabric cut:

    A: 3 pieces 11 cm x 11 cm

    B: 2 pieces 27 cm x 7 cm

4 Baste cream fabric squares to the back of Hardanger pieces A, B, C, and D. Baste a square of the pink fabric to the back of piece E, with the right side of pink fabric facing the wrong side of the Hardanger.

5 Machine sew all patches together, following the piecing diagrams below. Press seam allowances open at the back as you go.

6 With right sides together, join the ends of the three long pieces of main fabric together to form one

large loop for the frill. Press seam allowances open.

7 On right side of frill fabric, position straight edge of lace 1.5 cm from the edge. Pin and baste in position. Where ends of lace meet, make seam allowance of 7 mm, and carefully hand sew together with seam allowance at back of lace. Trim any excess lace. Using a short stitch length on sewing machine, with thread to match lace, sew 1-2 mm from the inside edge of lace to attach to frill.

8 Fold frill in half, with wrong sides together. Using a long stitch length on the sewing machine, stitch 1cm and then 2 cm from unfinished edge. These lines of stitching will form the gathering threads.

PIECING DIAGRAMS

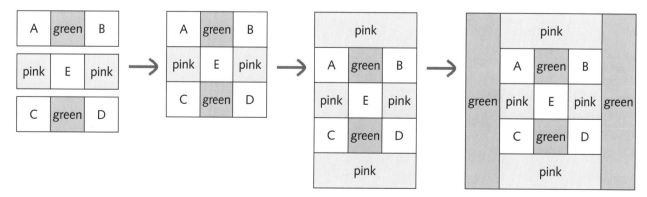

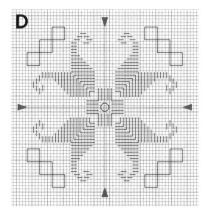

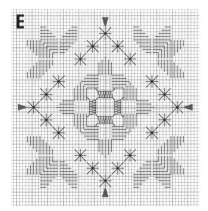

9 Divide frill into four equal parts, marking each section with a pin or basting stitches. With right sides of cushion front and frill facing each other, and raw edges together, match frill markings to the centre of each edge of the patched cushion front. Pin in place. Pull up gathering threads on frill to fit each quarter of the cushion edges, easing a little extra fullness into the corners. Pin and baste in position.

10 On the back of each of the two remaining pieces of green fabric (23.5 cm x 35 cm), align the interfacing with one of the long edges. Press in place. Use a zigzag stitch or overlock to finish the interfaced edge. Fold along the edge of the interfacing to form facing to strengthen buttonholes. Press.

11 On the front of one of the buttonhole facings sew buttonholes in positions as marked on the

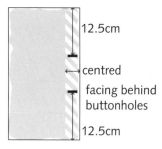

diagram. Cut buttonholes to allow buttons to pass through.

12 To create the back of the cushion, place the two pieces of fabric, face up, side by side, with facings in the centre. Overlap the facings by 4cm with buttonholed facing on top. At the edges of the fabric, baste overlapped sections together. Through the buttonholes, mark the button positions and sew in place on lower facing.

13 Lay back of cushion face down over right side of cushion front and frill. Pin and baste in position.

14 Machine sew around the edge. Turn inside out and check that the frill sits correctly. Unpick and adjust sections where necessary. Overlock or zigzag raw edges to neaten. Remove gathering threads.

15 Turn cushion cover right side out. Stuff with cushion insert, making sure cushion insert corners match with the cushion cover corners. Button up at back.

Hardanger box

This keepsake box with a padded Hardanger lid would take pride of place on the dressing table. The needleweaving centre is surrounded by satin stitch motifs and Algerian eyelets.

DIFFICULTY Beginner
FINISHED SIZE 15 cm diameter

See page 55 for a coloured photograph of this project.

MATERIALS
- 20 cm x 20 cm cream Hardanger fabric, 22 count
- 1 skein No. 5 DMC pearl cotton, colour 712 (cream)
- 1 ball No. 8 DMC pearl cotton, colour 712 (cream)
- No. 24 tapestry needle
- 15 cm diameter papier-mâché box
- craft glue (clear, fast drying)
- folk art paint, dark blue
- water based varnish
- paintbrush
- 1 m x 1 cm-wide braid, dark blue
- 20 cm x 20 cm satin lining fabric, dark blue
- 15 cm x 15 cm thick polyester wadding
- machine sewing thread
- 15cm x 15cm medium-weight card

❶ *The quantities of some threads used in this project are minimal. Use leftovers from other projects if you have them.*

STITCHES USED
Satin stitch, Algerian eyelets, needleweaving bars.

EMBROIDERY
1 Fold fabric in half to find the centre. Run a line of tacking along each fold. The lines of tacking form the centre guides for the embroidery.

2 Work all satin stitch in the No. 5 pearl cotton.

3 Work all Algerian eyelets and needleweaving in the No. 8 pearl cotton.

4 Remove the tacking.

CONSTRUCTION
1 Paint the box base inside and out with the folk art paint. Paint the sides and inside of the lid. Leave the

top of the lid unpainted. Repeat with a second coat if necessary. Follow manufacturer's instructions for drying and recoat times.

2 Varnish painted surfaces according to manufacturer's instructions.

3 Cut a circle of wadding, 15 cm in diameter.

4 Cut a circle from the medium-weight card, 14.8 cm in diameter. Run a line of craft glue around the edge of the card. Attach wadding.

5 Cut a circle from the lining fabric, 20 cm in diameter.

6 Using the machine sewing thread, sew a line of small running stitch as a gathering thread 1cm from the edge of the fabric. Leave the ends of the thread hanging loose.

7 Place the lining over the wadding. Draw the gathering thread up tightly on the underside of the card. Tie ends off securely.

8 With embroidery carefully centred, cut a 20 cm circle from the Hardanger fabric. Repeat gathering as for the lining, fitting the embroidery over the lined, padded side of the card. Make sure the embroidery is centred on the padded top. Adjust if necessary.

9 Glue the padded top to the box lid using craft glue. To make sure the edges of the padded top adhere well to the lid, it may be helpful to place it under a weighty object such as a book, until the glue is dry.

10 With a thin line of glue, carefully glue approximately half the length of braid around the top of the lid to cover the gap between the box lid and the padded top. To neaten the ends of the braid, fold the first 5mm back against itself with wrong sides together and glue it. At the end, cut off 5 mm more than is needed and glue under as for the beginning. Make sure the glue does not ooze out or leave strings.

11 Glue the remaining braid around the base of the box.

Hand towel

This hand towel makes a beautiful addition to the bathroom. The central diamond of dove's eye needleweaving is flanked by tulips and smaller diamonds. Four-sided stitch borders the design.

DIFFICULTY Beginner
FINISHED SIZE 35 cm x 50 cm

See page 52 for a coloured photograph of this project.

MATERIALS

- 38 cm x 56 cm white linen, 32 count (must be cut straight on the grain or the design will be crooked)
- 1 ball No. 8 DMC pearl cotton, white
- 1 ball No.12 DMC pearl cotton, white
- No. 24 tapestry needle
- machine sewing thread, white

STITCHES USED

Kloster blocks, satin stitch, eyelets, needleweaving bars, dove's eye stitch, four-sided stitch.

INSTRUCTIONS

❶ *The hemming of this hand towel requires a sewing machine and basic machine sewing skills.*

❶ *For full chart, work a mirror image on the other side of the vertical centre axis.*

1 On the long sides of the fabric create hems by folding over 5 mm, then another 10 mm and stitching 2 mm from the first fold.

2 Hem the two remaining sides by folding over 5 mm, then another 25 mm, and stitching 2 mm from the first fold.

3 Fold the short side in half to find its centre. With the front of the towel facing, run a line of counted tacking from the edge of the fabric. Secure the end of the thread when the tacking measures 10 cm.

4 Using the tacking, count 19 blocks of four threads (76 threads) from the hemmed edge and run a line of tacking across the fabric from side to side. The tacking lines are the centre guides for the embroidery.

5 With hems to the back, sew the kloster blocks and satin stitch with the No. 8 pearl cotton.

❶ *The remainder of the embroidery uses the No. 12 pearl cotton.*

6 Sew the four sections of four-sided stitch as a surface stitch with regular tension, working out from the centre diamond.

7 Sew all the eyelets over six threads rather than the usual four.

8 Complete all the needleweaving. Work the large diamond in straight lines or in a zigzag fashion. Either way will work satisfactorily in small areas of needleweaving.

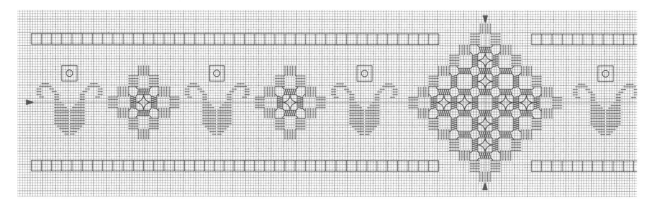

The design for this embroidery
was adapted from an antique
drawn thread sampler.
The Genevieve doily features
a variety of intricate, lacy
needleweaving stitches.
In a dark frame it makes
a stunning focal point.
Instructions page 78.

This beautiful star cushion features
Greek cross borders and pulled
thread work. The dark satin inner
cushion provides a dramatic
backdrop for the fine stitching.
Instructions page 62.

The delicate looking waterlily mini cushion would be perfect for a sunny bedroom. It features variegated silk thread, beading and lacy needleweaving.
Instructions page 75.

The delightful Trish runner features satin stitch tulips and a lacy needlewoven edge with dove's eyes. It would look very much at home on a sideboard or on the top of an antique upright piano.
Instructions page 72.

A ring of honeysuckle flowers graces the centre of this tablecloth. It is surrounded by lacy, open needleweaving featuring woven bars, dove's eye stitch and knotted picots.
Instructions page 68.

Decorated with a wide range of Hardanger stitches, this scissors case would make a treasured gift for the dedicated embroiderer. The case is made to suit 3 ½ inch embroidery scissors.
Instructions page 57.

Featuring intricate needleweaving, these gift cards will help to hone your skills and are sure to delight the recipient. They are also a great way to put scraps of material and thread to good use.
Instructions page 66.

This hand towel makes a beautiful addition to the bathroom. The central diamond of dove's eye needleweaving is flanked by tulips and smaller diamonds. Four-sided stitch borders the design.
Instructions page 48.

This sumptuous bolster is created by using an organza overlay on an evenweave fabric for the Hardanger. Although the stitches are simple, the organza overlay adds difficulty and will demand concentration while stitching, but the result is worth it! The organza used here is pale blue, shot with red. *Instructions page 80.*

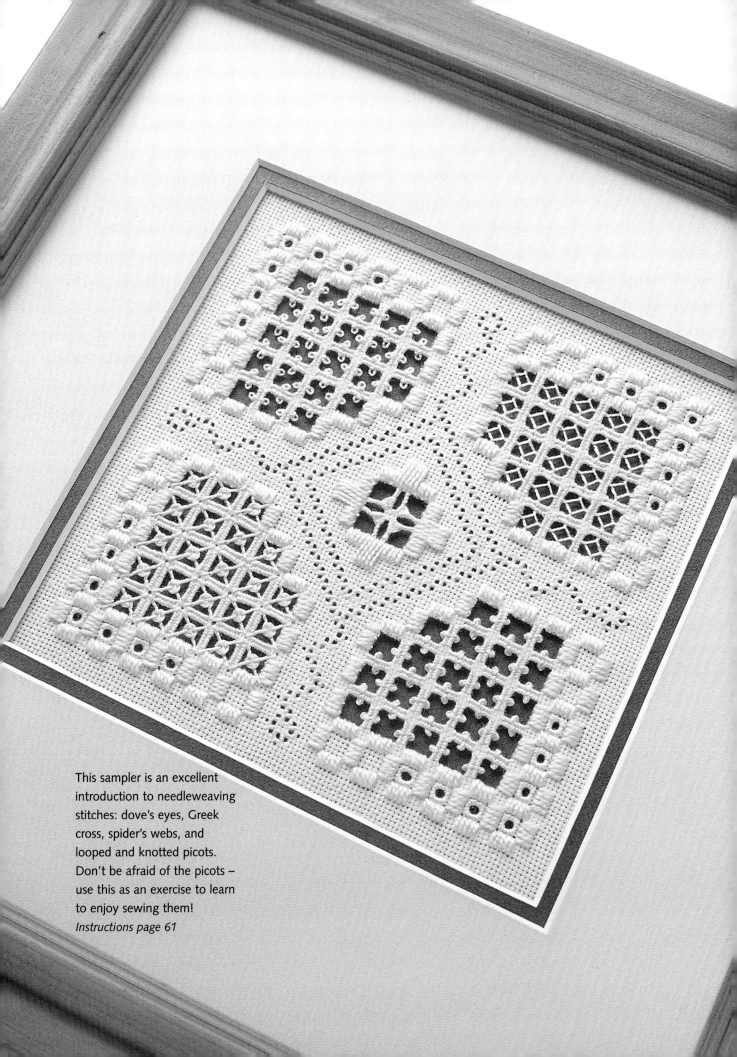

This sampler is an excellent
introduction to needleweaving
stitches: dove's eyes, Greek
cross, spider's webs, and
looped and knotted picots.
Don't be afraid of the picots –
use this as an exercise to learn
to enjoy sewing them!
Instructions page 61

Worked on a very fine count of fabric, delicate needleweaving and surface stitchery such as satin stitch and double cable stitch create a textured, dainty effect on the Claire doily.
Instructions page 70.

This keepsake box with a padded Hardanger lid would take pride of place on the dressing table. The needleweaving centre is surrounded by satin stitch motifs and Algerian eyelets.
Instructions page 46.

A great gift in itself, this stocking is perfect for some special Christmas treats. To personalise it, you could embroider the owner's name on the cuff at the back of the stocking.
Instructions page 59.

This cushion beautifully combines patchwork and Hardanger. The outer Hardanger designs feature surface stitchery and are highlighted in green to match the patchwork. The centre design features elegant cream on cream. *Instructions page 43.*

With looped picots and dove's eye needleweaving, the Karen doily would make a beautiful tray mat for coffee with friends. Stranded embroidery cotton is used to create a softer look than pearl cotton. *Instructions page 64.*

Scissors case

Decorated with a wide range of Hardanger stitches, this scissors case would make a treasured gift for the dedicated embroiderer. The case is made to suit 3½ inch embroidery scissors.

DIFFICULTY Beginner
FINISHED SIZE 8 cm x 11 cm

See page 52 for a coloured photograph of this project.

MATERIALS
- 10 cm x 30 cm blue-grey Lugana, 25 count
- 1 skein DMC stranded cotton, colour 932 (blue)
- 1 skein No. 5 DMC pearl cotton, white
- 1 ball No. 8 DMC pearl cotton, white
- No. 24 tapestry needle
- 10 cm x 30 cm white buckram
- 10 cm blue-grey satin fabric
- 1 white pearl bead, 6 mm diameter
- 1m blue-grey cord, 3 mm diameter
- machine sewing thread to match fabric

❶ *The quantities of some threads used in this project are minimal. Use leftovers from other projects if you have them.*

STITCHES USED
Kloster blocks, satin stitch, needleweaving bars, Algerian eyelets, double cable stitch.

EMBROIDERY
1 Fold the long side of the Lugana into three equal sections. Along one of the folds, run a line of tacking. Fold the short side in half. Run a line of tacking down the fold. The two lines of tacking form the centre guides for the embroidery.

2 Begin by working all the kloster blocks and satin stitch in the No. 5 pearl cotton.

3 Work all the eyelets and Algerian eyelets with two strands of the stranded cotton.

4 Work the cable stitch in the No. 8 pearl cotton.

5 Cut and remove the threads from the centre diamond and work the needle weaving with the No. 8 pearl cotton.

CONSTRUCTION
1 Photocopy the cutting pattern at 200 per cent. Cut one pattern piece from the satin fabric and one from the buckram.

2 Lay the enlarged cutting pattern over the Hardanger, carefully matching the dots to the lines of tacking. Check that the embroidery sits well within the cutting area. Cut the Lugana according to the pattern.

3 Baste the Hardanger to the satin fabric 6 mm from the edge. The back of the Hardanger should face the front of the satin.

4 Lay the Hardanger and lining face down on the buckram. Machine stitch around the edge with 1 cm seam allowance, leaving the seam open between the stars (marked on the cutting pattern). Trim the buckram to 4 mm. Clip corners and curves and turn inside out. Press.

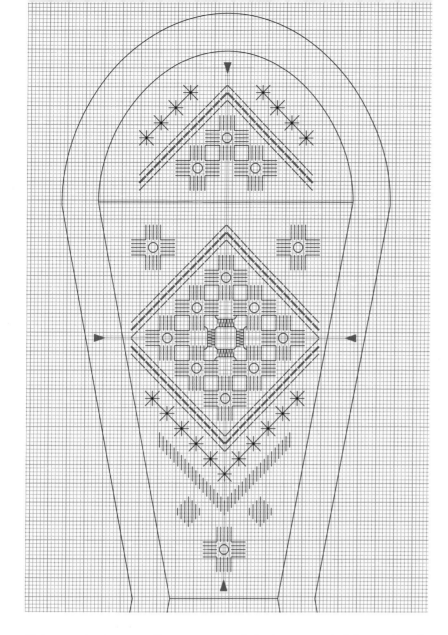

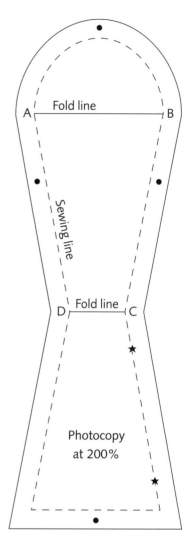

❶ *Because buckram is stiff, turning it inside out will be difficult. It is possible, so be persistent!*

5 Close the opening between the stars with whip stitch.

6 Fold the triangular end up to meet the middle section. Whip stitch along each side to form a pocket. The stitches need to be very short so that the point of the embroidery scissors cannot slip out the side seam.

7 Sew cord around the edge of the case with whip stitch. Begin by fastening one end of the cord inside the top of the case at A (as marked on cutting pattern). Attach around the curved flap. At B, leave a small gap in the stitching, large enough to pass the end of the cord through later. Continue stitching the cord down the side to C, across the bottom to D, and up the other side to A. When the stitching meets the beginning of the cord at A, take a few strong stitches to fasten it securely. Finish off thread.

8 Taking the loose end of the cord, thread it through the gap in the stitching at B. Secure the end inside the top of the case using a number of strong stitches.

9 Fold down the flap, and where the end of it meets the main body of the case, sew on the bead.

10 On the end of the flap section of the cover make a buttonhole loop as follows to fit around the bead. Using two strands of the stranded cotton, loop the thread three times, and tightly buttonhole stitch the loop.

11 Remove the tacking guides for the Hardanger embroidery.

Christmas stocking

A great gift in itself, this stocking is perfect for some special Christmas treats. To personalise it, you could embroider the owner's name on the cuff at the back of the stocking.

DIFFICULTY Beginner
FINISHED SIZE 20 cm x 30 cm

See page 55 for a coloured photograph of this project.

MATERIALS
- 35 cm x 12.5 cm white Hardanger fabric, 22 count
- 1 skein No. 5 DMC pearl cotton, white
- 1 ball of No. 8 DMC pearl cotton, white
- 1 skein DMC stranded cotton, colour 5282 (gold)
- 1 skein DMC stranded cotton, colour 817 (red)
- red seed beads
- No. 24 tapestry needle
- beading needle
- 35 cm x 12.5 cm white cotton fabric
- 40 cm dark green quilted fabric
- sewing machine thread, dark green and white
- 1 m gold cord, approximately 9 mm diameter

❶ *The quantities of some threads used in this project are minimal. Use leftovers from other projects if you have them.*

STITCHES USED
Kloster blocks, satin stitch, eyelets, Algerian eyelets, double cable stitch, beading.

EMBROIDERY
1 Fold short side of Hardanger fabric in half. Run a line of tacking along the fold. Measure 9.5 cm from one of the short ends of the fabric and run a line of tacking perpendicular to the first. The tacking will be the centre guides for the embroidery.

2 Work the kloster blocks and satin stitch stars in the white No .5 pearl cotton.

3 Stitch the eyelets in white No. 8 pearl cotton.

4 Work the double cable stitch in one strand of the red cotton.

5 Using one strand of the gold cotton stitch all Algerian eyelets.

6 Using one strand of the red cotton and the beading needle sew a single bead in the centre of each Algerian eyelet in the outer rows.

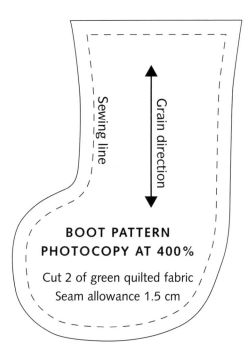

BOOT PATTERN
PHOTOCOPY AT 400%

Cut 2 of green quilted fabric
Seam allowance 1.5 cm

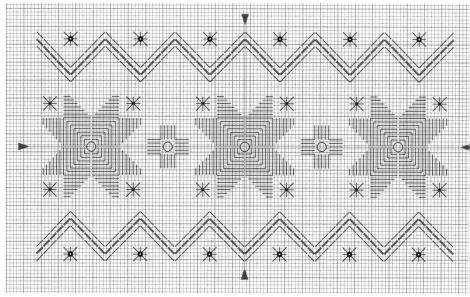

CONSTRUCTION

❶ *All seam allowances of 1.5 cm
are included in pattern pieces.*

1 Place Hardanger fabric right side up with embroidery to the right. Lay the white cotton fabric over the top, face down.

2 Sew the two fabrics together along the bottom edge.

3 Open out along the seam. Press. Fold in half the other way with right sides of fabric together.

4 Sew a seam down the side to create a tube. To create the cuff, fold the tube back on itself so that the cotton fabric is inside the tube and the Hardanger fabric faces outwards.

5 Photocopy the cutting pattern for the boot at 400 per cent onto A3 paper. Fold the green quilted fabric in half, and from it cut two boot pieces using the enlarged pattern.

6 With right sides together, stitch around the bottom of the two boot pieces. Trim seams to 7 mm. Overcast, zigzag or overlock seams on straight upper sections of boot to neaten. Clip curves in the lower section of the boot.

7 Turn the cuff inside out so that the Hardanger faces inwards and the cotton faces outwards. Slip it over the top of the boot.

8 Match the unfinished edge of the cuff with the unfinished edge of the boot, with cuff seam matched to back seam of boot. Sew a seam around the unfinished edges. Overcast, zigzag or overlock edge to neaten.

9 Turn the boot section so that right side faces out, and fold the cuff down over the top of boot.

10 Fasten one end of the cord, hiding it underneath the bottom of the cuff at the back seam. Slip stitch the cord around the bottom of the

cuff. Where the cord meets, cut it allowing 1.5 cm extra for finishing the end. Fasten and overcast both ends to neaten so that they will not fray.

11 With the remainder of the cord, fasten one end inside the boot, 3 cm from the top at the back seam. Slip stitch the cord around the top of the boot. When the cord meets, take several strong stitches through both the cord and the top of the boot to fasten it securely in place.

12 Loop the remainder of the cord up to create a hanging loop. Bring the end back down to meet the beginning and secure inside the boot. Overcast both ends to neaten and secure so that they will not fray.

Square sampler

This sampler is an excellent introduction to needleweaving stitches: dove's eyes, Greek cross, spider's webs, and looped and knotted picots. Don't be afraid of the picots – use this as an exercise to learn to enjoy stitching them!

DIFFICULTY Intermediate
FINISHED SIZE 13 cm x 13 cm

See page 54 for a coloured photograph of this project.

MATERIALS

- 20 cm x 20 cm cream Hardanger fabric, 22 count
- 1 skein No. 5 DMC pearl cotton, colour 712 (cream)
- 1 ball No. 8 DMC pearl cotton, colour 712 (cream)
- No. 24 tapestry needle

STITCHES USED

Kloster blocks, satin stitch, eyelets, needleweaving bars, knotted picots, dove's eye stitch, looped picots, spider's webs, Greek cross, faggot stitch.

INSTRUCTIONS

1 Stitch satin stitch in the centre using No. 5 pearl cotton.

2 Stitch kloster blocks in No. 5 pearl cotton.

3 Work all eyelets using No .8 pearl cotton.

4 Work all faggot stitch using No. 8 pearl cotton.

5 Work the Greek cross in the centre, using No. 8 pearl cotton.

6 Work all needleweaving in No. 8 pearl cotton using the straight line method of ordering the stitching. Follow the chart for placement of dove's eyes, knotted picots, spider's webs and looped picots.

7 Frame sampler as desired.

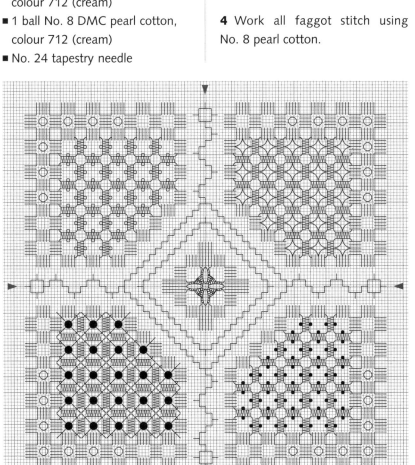

Star cushion

This beautiful cushion features Greek cross borders and pulled thread work. The dark satin inner cushion provides a dramatic backdrop for the fine stitching.

DIFFICULTY Intermediate
FINISHED SIZE 29 cm x 29 cm

See page 49 for a coloured photograph of this project.

MATERIALS

- 2 pieces 30 cm x 30 cm cream linen, 28 count
- 2 skeins No. 5 DMC pearl cotton, colour 712 (cream)
- 1 ball No. 8 DMC pearl cotton, colour 712 (cream)
- 1 skein DMC stranded embroidery cotton, colour 712 (cream)
- No. 24 tapestry needle
- 30 cm x 30 cm dark coloured satin fabric, 2 pieces
- 1.3 m cord trim, cord approximately 9 mm diameter
- machine sewing threads to match linen and satin fabric
- 30 cm cushion insert

STITCHES USED

Kloster blocks, satin stitch, eyelets, Greek cross border, four-sided stitch.

EMBROIDERY

❶ *For the full chart, work mirror images of the design in each of the other three quarters.*

1 Work all kloster blocks using No. 5 pearl cotton.

2 Work the eyelets within the

kloster block groupings using the No. 8 pearl cotton.

3 Using one strand of stranded embroidery cotton, complete the sections of four-sided stitch, using tight tension to create the pulled thread version of the stitch.

4 Work the Greek cross borders in the No. 8 pearl cotton.

5 Work all satin stitch using the No. 5 pearl cotton.

6 Work the eyelets in the centre of the stars using the No. 8 pearl cotton.

CONSTRUCTION

❶ *If the cord you are using is attached to an edging of flat braid, omit step 7. If it is the cord only, omit steps 1 and 6.*

1 With the embroidered cushion front face up, lay the braid, with cord toward the centre, around the edge of the fabric. Overlap the ends of the braid in the middle of one of the sides, curving the raw ends into the seam area (see diagram) so that they will be concealed when sewn.

Baste braid in place, easing extra fullness into the corners.

2 With right sides together, sew a 1.5 cm seam around the edges of the cushion front and back. Leave a 15 cm gap in one of the sides. Turn the cushion cover right side out.

3 Place the two pieces of satin lining fabric with right sides together and sew a 1.5 cm seam around the edges. Leave a 15 cm opening in one of the sides. Turn the lining right side out through the opening.

4 Insert the cushion insert into the satin lining cushion, making sure that the corners of the insert match up with the satin cover. Close the gap with slip stitch.

5 Insert the satin cushion into the embroidered cover, matching corners with corners.

6 Slip stitch to close the gap.

7 Slip stitch most of the gap closed, leaving an opening of 2 cm. Insert one end of the cord into the gap. Use a few small stitches to secure the end in place. Laying the cord around the edge of the cushion, whip stitch it in place. Insert the other end of the braid into the gap, overlapping it over the previous end. Slipstitch the gap closed, enclosing the ends of the braid.

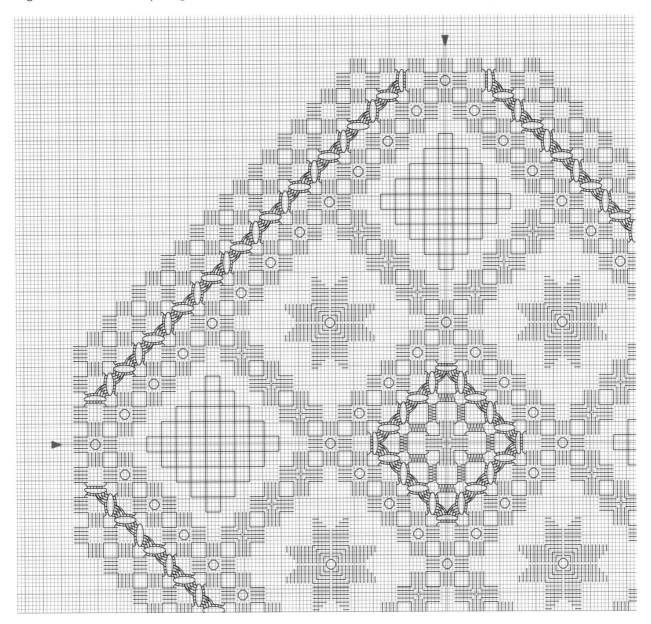

Karen doily

With looped picots and dove's eye needleweaving, this delicate doily would make a beautiful tray mat for coffee with friends. Stranded embroidery cotton is used to create a softer, finer look than pearl cotton.

DIFFICULTY Intermediate
FINISHED SIZE 31 cm x 27 cm

See page 56 for a coloured photograph of this project.

MATERIALS
- 40 cm x 30 cm white linen, 30 count
- 4 skeins stranded embroidery cotton, white
- No. 24 tapestry needle

STITCHES USED
Kloster blocks, eyelets, buttonhole edge, needleweaving bars, looped picots, dove's eye stitch, faggot stitch.

INSTRUCTIONS

❶ *For the full chart, work mirror images of the design in each of the other three quarters.*

1 Using three strands of the embroidery cotton, stitch all the kloster blocks.

2 Work the buttonhole edge using three strands of embroidery cotton.

3 Use two strands of embroidery thread to work the eyelets.

4 Work the line of faggot stitch, using one strand of embroidery cotton.

5 Stitch all needleweaving using one strand of embroidery cotton.

6 Carefully cut the finished embroidery from the surrounding fabric, remembering to work slowly and carefully, from the back of the fabric.

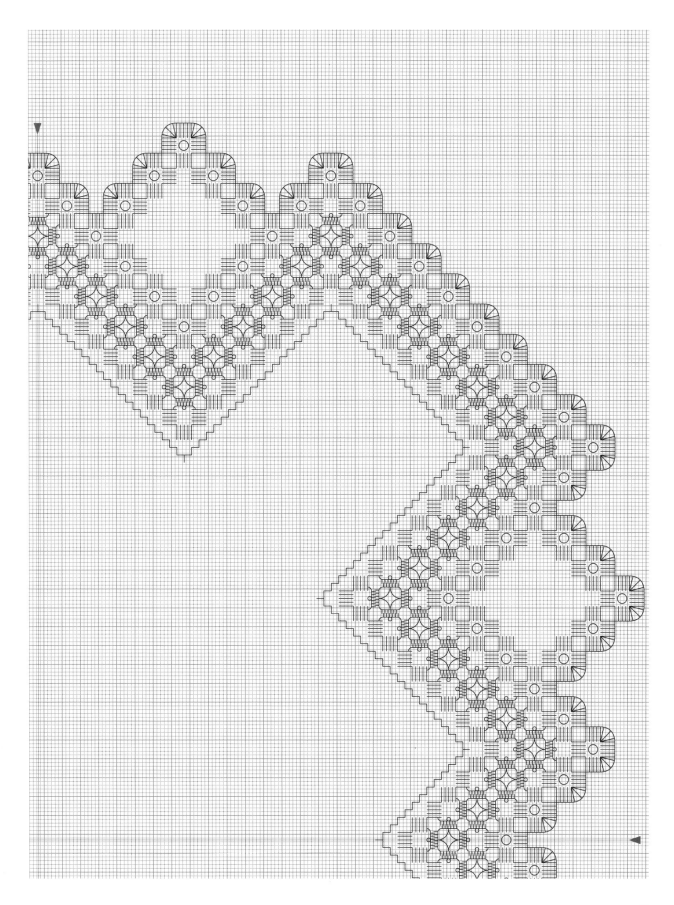

Gift cards

Featuring intricate needleweaving, these gift cards will help to develop your skills and are sure to delight the recipient. They are also a great way to put scraps of material and thread to good use.

DIFFICULTY Intermediate
FINISHED SIZES
Square embroidery 4 cm x 4 cm
Diamond embroidery 6 cm x 6 cm

See page 52 for a coloured photograph of this project.

MATERIALS
Square embroidery
- 10 cm x 10 cm pale coloured linen, 28 count
- 1 skein No. 5 DMC pearl cotton, colour 712 (cream)
- 1 ball No. 8 DMC pearl cotton, colour 712 (cream)
- pre-purchased window card, to suit
- No. 24 tapestry needle

Diamond embroidery
- 12 cm x 12 cm white linen, 30 count
- 1 ball No. 8 DMC pearl cotton, white
- 1 ball No. 12 DMC pearl cotton, white
- pre-purchased card to suit
- No. 24 tapestry needle

❶ *The quantities of threads used in this project are minimal. Use leftovers from other projects if you have them. You can also use leftover scraps of fabric. Keep in mind that if using a different count of fabric, the finished size will be different.*

STITCHES USED
Square embroidery
Satin stitch, four-sided stitch, Algerian eyelets, needleweaving bars, Greek cross, dove's eye stitch.

Diamond embroidery
Kloster blocks, eyelets, buttonhole edge, needleweaving bars, spider's web, dove's eye stitch, triangular webs with buttonhole bars.

SQUARE EMBROIDERY
1 Work all the satin stitch in No.5 pearl cotton.

2 Work the four-sided stitch as a pulled thread stitch, using the No.8 pearl cotton. Make sure that it is worked over groups of only two threads rather than the usual four.

❶ *Work all needleweaving in the No. 8 pearl cotton.*

3 Weave all four bars of row 1. Refer to the square embroidery stitching order diagram.

4 Take the thread through the back of the adjacent satin stitch and bring it out in the first bar of row 2. Weave the first bar, working a dove's eye stitch in the corner space. Work an Algerian eyelet in the woven square. Weave the next three bars.

5 Repeat for row 3.

6 Take the thread through the back of the satin stitch to row 4.

SQUARE EMBROIDERY CHART

Weave the first bar, completing a dove's eye stitch in the corner space. Work an Algerian eyelet in the woven square. Weave the next two bars. Work an Algerian eyelet in the woven square. Weave the last bar, working a dove's eye stitch in the corner space.

7 Take the thread through the back of the satin stitch to row 5. Weave the first bar, working dove's eye stitches on either side. Lace the thread behind the next two bars. Weave the final bar of the row with dove's eye stitches on either side.

8 Take the thread through the back of the satin stitch to row 6. Weave the first bar, working a dove's eye stitch on either side. Lace behind the next two bars. Secure the thread behind the woven square. Work a Greek cross in the centre of the needleweaving area, catching in the laced threads

as you sew. Weave the final bar with a dove's eye stitch on either side. Secure the thread in the back of the satin stitch.

❶ *To attach the embroidery to the card, use a thin line of craft glue inside the card, close to the edges of the window. Lay the embroidery face down over the back of the window so that the front shows through, making sure it is centred over the hole. Keep the embroidery taut as you press it onto the glue. Turn the card over and check the positioning. Adjust as necessary.*

DIAMOND EMBROIDERY

1 Work all kloster blocks and the buttonhole edge using the No.8 pearl cotton.

2 Use the No. 12 pearl cotton to embroider the eyelets.

3 Work all needleweaving in the No.12 pearl cotton. This design could be worked using either the zigzag method or the straight lines method.

4 Carefully cut the embroidery from the surrounding fabric.

❶ *To attach the embroidery to the card, you will need to sew it on. Use a fine thread in white (or in a colour that blends with the embroidery and fabric). Make a small, invisible stitch through the card and the embroidery in each of the corners and one through the middle. Tie off the ends of the thread on the back so that it is secure.*

❶ *If preferred, you could make your own cards to suit the embroideries, rather than buying ready-made ones.*

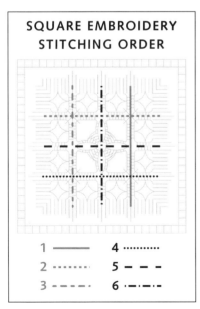

SQUARE EMBROIDERY STITCHING ORDER

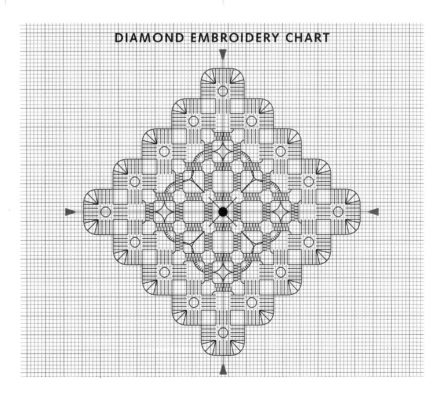

DIAMOND EMBROIDERY CHART

Honeysuckle tablecloth

A ring of honeysuckle flowers graces the centre of this tablecloth. It is surrounded by lacy, open needleweaving featuring woven bars, dove's eye stitch, and knotted picots.

DIFFICULTY Intermediate
FINISHED SIZE 80 cm x 80 cm

See page 51 for a coloured photograph of this project.

MATERIALS

- 90 cm x 90 cm white Lugana, 25 count (must be cut straight on the grain or the embroidery will be crooked)
- 1 ball No. 8 DMC pearl cotton, white
- 4 skeins No. 5 DMC pearl cotton, white
- No. 24 tapestry needle
- machine sewing thread, white
- water-soluble fabric marker

STITCHES USED

Kloster blocks, satin stitch, eyelets, needleweaving bars, dove's eye stitch, knotted picots.

❗ *It is wise to hem this project first so that the embroidery is centred on the cloth.*

CONSTRUCTION

1 Fold in 6 mm along each side of the fabric. Press. Fold in another 20 mm along each side. Press. Keep hems folded.

2 Using a water-soluble marker, mark the intersection of inner edges of the hems, as shown in the diagram.

3 Unfold hems. Make a fold through the two marked points diagonally across the corner. The crease is the stitching line for the mitre. Unfold.

4 Refold 6 mm fold as in step 1.

5 With right sides together, fold fabric diagonally, through the corner. Sew along the mitre stitching line, keeping 6mm fold in place.

6 Trim the mitre seam allowance to 6 mm. Turn the corner the right way out, with seam open flat and 6 mm fold tucked inside hem.

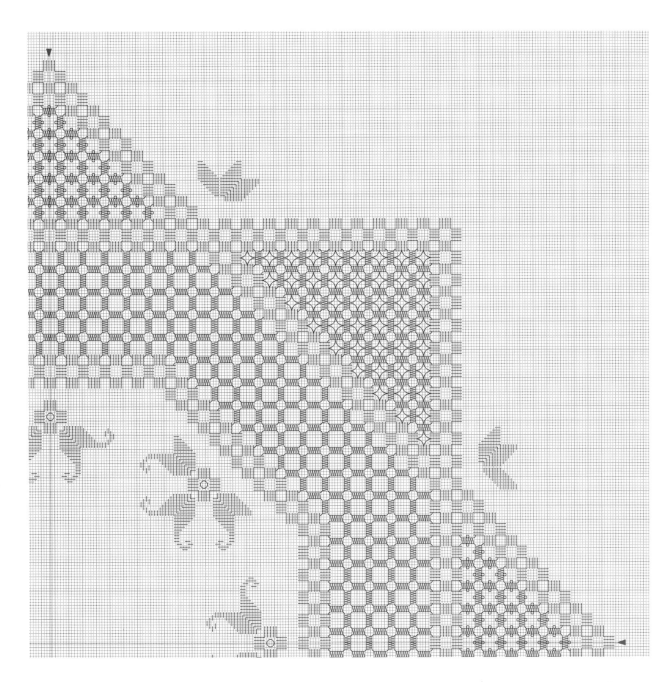

7 Repeat for other three corners.

8 Machine sew 2 mm from the inside edge of the hem.

9 Remove the water-soluble marker according to the manufacturer's directions.

EMBROIDERY

❶ *For the full chart, work mirror images of the design in each of the other three quarters.*

1 Fold tablecloth in half both ways. Run a line of tacking along each fold, to form the centre guide for the embroidery.

2 With hems to the back, work all kloster blocks and satin stitch in the No. 5 pearl cotton.

3 Work all eyelets in the No. 8 pearl cotton.

4 Work all needleweaving in the No.8 pearl cotton, positioning the filling stitches as on the chart.

5 Remove tacking.

Claire doily

Worked on a very fine count of fabric, delicate needleweaving and surface stitchery such as satin stitch and double cable stitch create a textured, dainty effect on this doily.

DIFFICULTY Advanced
FINISHED SIZE 33 cm x 33 cm

See page 55 for a coloured photograph of this project.

MATERIALS
- 40 cm x 40 cm white linen, 32 count
- 1 ball No. 8 DMC pearl cotton, white
- 1 ball No. 12 DMC pearl cotton, white
- No. 24 tapestry needle

STITCHES USED
Kloster blocks, satin stitch, needleweaving bars, spider's webs, Greek cross, spider's webs with eyelets, buttonhole edge, double cable stitch.

INSTRUCTIONS
1 Stitch all kloster blocks and satin stitch and the buttonhole edge using the No. 8 pearl cotton.

2 Work the centre diamond and outer border of needleweaving using the No. 12 pearl cotton.

3 Using the No. 12 pearl cotton, work the four sections of needle-weaving with Greek crosses.

4 Work the eight spider's webs with eyelets using the No. 12 pearl cotton.

5 Work all double cable stitch using the No. 12 pearl cotton.

6 Carefully cut the embroidery from the surrounding fabric.

Trish runner

This delightful runner features satin stitch tulips and a lacy needlewoven edge with a dove's eye border. It would look very much at home on a sideboard or on the top of an antique upright piano.

DIFFICULTY Advanced
FINISHED SIZE 68 cm x 20 cm

See page 50 for a coloured photograph of this project.

MATERIALS
- 80 cm x 30 cm cream linen, 28 count
- 3 skeins No. 5 DMC pearl cotton, colour 712 (cream)
- 2 balls No. 8 DMC pearl cotton, colour 712 (cream)
- No. 24 tapestry needle

STITCHES USED
Kloster blocks, satin stitch, eyelets, needleweaving bars, knotted picots, dove's eye stitch, lacy buttonhole edge, dove's eye in a wrapped circle.

INSTRUCTIONS

❶ *See page 74 for chart.*

❶ *The diagram on the right shows how many times each section of the chart needs to be repeated to create the full design. There are four diamond sections.*

1 Stitch all kloster blocks and satin stitch in the No. 5 pearl cotton.

2 Stitch all eyelets within the kloster blocks, using the No. 8 pearl cotton.

3 The tulip flower eyelets cover six threads instead of the usual four. Stitch in No. 8 pearl cotton.

4 Complete the needleweaving in the four diamonds using the No. 8 pearl cotton.

5 Work the lacy edge needleweaving, including the strengthening threads, according to the instructions on page 35. Once the strengthening threads are in place, proceed with the needleweaving, working in straight lines, rather than zigzagging.

6 Cut the finished Hardanger from the surrounding fabric. Work slowly and carefully from the back of the fabric.

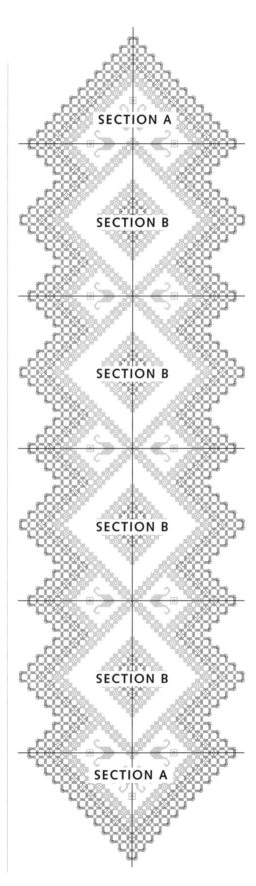

SECTION A

SECTION B

SECTION B

SECTION B

SECTION B

SECTION A

SECTION A

SECTION B

Waterlily mini cushion

This delicate looking cushion would be perfect for a sunny bedroom. It features soft shades of variegated silk thread, antique glass beads and intricate needleweaving.

DIFFICULTY Advanced
FINISHED SIZE 25 cm x 25 cm

See page 51 for a coloured photograph of this project.

MATERIALS

- 2 pieces 28 cm x 28 cm "Waterlily" Permin linen, 28 count
- 1 skein Gumnut Yarns Buds silk, colour 626
- 1 skein DMC stranded cotton, colour 3072
- Mill Hill antique glass beads, colour 03028
- No.24 tapestry needle
- beading needle
- polyester filling
- 2 pieces 20 cm x 20 cm pale green satin fabric
- machine sewing thread to match

STITCHES USED

Kloster blocks, satin stitch, eyelets, needleweaving bars, looped picots with twisted Y, dove's eye stitch, looped picots, beading.

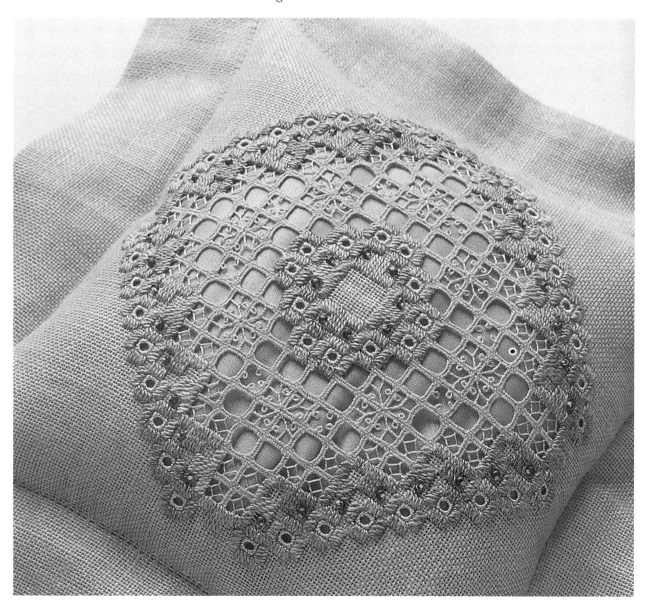

EMBROIDERY

1 Work all satin stitch and kloster blocks in one strand of the silk.

2 Using two strands of the stranded cotton, work all eyelets.

3 Use one strand of the stranded cotton to work the needleweaving. Follow the order shown in the stitching order diagram.

❶ *When you come to the twisted Y with looped picot combinations, use the lacing method (see page 26) so that you can work the whole combination in one go.*

4 To sew on the beads, use two strands of stranded cotton with the beading needle. Follow the chart for bead positioning.

CONSTRUCTION

❶ *All seam allowances of 1.5 cm included in pattern pieces.*

1 Place the two linen squares with right sides together. Sew around the edges, leaving a 12 cm gap in the middle of one side. Clip the corners and turn right side out. Press.

2 To create the cushion flange, sew 4 cm in from the edges, leaving a 12 cm gap in the corresponding position to the previous opening.

3 Place the two pieces of lining fabric with right sides together. Sew around the edges, leaving an 8 cm gap in one side. Clip the corners and turn right side out.

4 Fill the lining cushion with the polyester filling, taking care to fill out the corners properly. Do not

overstuff the cushion. Slip stitch the opening closed.

5 Insert the lining cushion into the linen cushion cover, making sure the inner cushion corners match up with and fill the corners of the cushion cover.

6 Working from the front, back-stitch neatly to close the gap in the line of stitching 4 cm from the edge.

7 Ladder stitch the edge of the flange to close the outer opening.

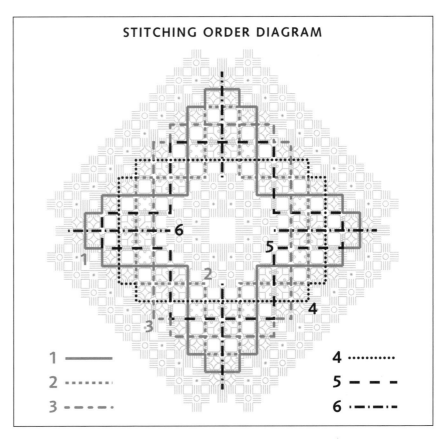

STITCHING ORDER DIAGRAM

1 —————
2 ·····················
3 — — — —·

4 ·····················
5 — — — —
6 ·—·—·—·

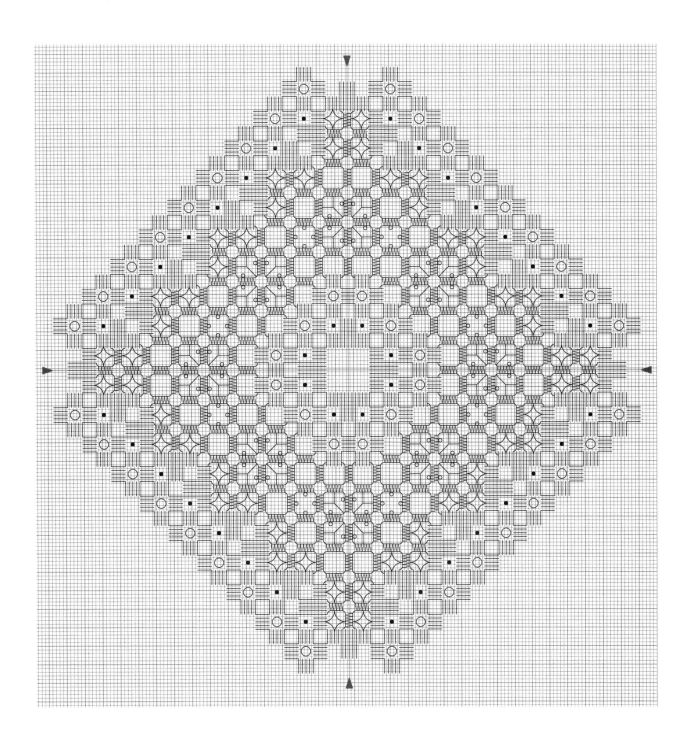

Genevieve framed doily

The design for this embroidery was adapted from an antique drawn thread sampler. The doily features a variety of intricate, lacy needleweaving stitches. In a dark frame it makes a stunning focal point.

DIFFICULTY Advanced
FINISHED SIZE 13.5cm x 13.5cm

See page 49 for a coloured photograph of this project.

MATERIALS
- 25 cm x 25 cm white linen, 32 count
- 3 skeins DMC stranded embroidery cotton, white
- No. 24 tapestry needle

STITCHES USED
Kloster blocks, satin stitch, faggot stitch, dove's eye in a wrapped circle, spider's web, lacy buttonhole edge.

INSTRUCTIONS
1 Stitch all kloster blocks and satin stitch using three strands of cotton.

2 Work faggot stitch using one strand of embroidery cotton.

3 Work all needleweaving in the centre section using one strand of embroidery cotton. Work in zigzags rather than straight lines. When working the dove's eyes, first stitch the wrapped bars to create the circles. When the fourth side of each circle has been wrapped, work the centre dove's eye before moving on to the next bar.

4 After laying the strengthening threads, stitch the lacy buttonhole edge using two strands of embroidery cotton. Work in straight lines, rather than zigzagging.

5 Cut the finished Hardanger from the surrounding fabric. Work slowly and carefully, from the back of the fabric.

Organza bolster

This sumptuous bolster is created by using an organza overlay on an evenweave fabric for the Hardanger. Although the stitches are simple, the organza overlay adds difficulty and will demand concentration while stitching, but the result is worth it! The organza used here is pale blue shot with red.

DIFFICULTY Advanced

FINISHED SIZE 46 cm x 15 cm

See page 53 for a coloured photograph of this project.

MATERIALS
- 46 cm x 20 cm white Lugana, 25 count
- 60 cm organza (140 cm wide)
- 50 cm white polycotton (lining)
- 2 skeins No. 5 pearl cotton, to match organza (DMC 3041 used here)
- 1 skein stranded embroidery cotton, to match organza (DMC 3041 used here)
- No. 24 tapestry needle
- beading needle
- 5 grams seed beads to match organza
- machine sewing threads to match organza and lining
- 1 m medium-weight piping cord
- 30 cm zip to match organza
- 2 x 22 mm buttons
- embroidery hoop, 15 cm diameter

- polyester filling
- bodkin or stiletto

STITCHES USED

Kloster blocks, satin stitch, eyelets, beading.

FABRIC CUTTING INSTRUCTIONS

From the organza cut:

1 main piece: 20 cm x 46 cm

2 ruched sections: 16 cm x 80 cm

2 end sections: 10 cm x 46 cm

2 bias strips: 4 cm x 50 cm

From the lining fabric cut:

2 ruched section linings:
  16 cm x 46 cm

1 piece: 46 cm x 46 cm

2 circles: 17 cm diameter

EMBROIDERY

❶ *The Hardanger stitching is done through the organza, using the backing of Lugana for the stitch placement. It can be difficult to see through the organza, so it may be helpful to illuminate the work from below. Alternatively, after some practice, you may find it easier to work the embroidery from the back, regularly checking that the stitches are correct on the front.*

❶ *For the full chart, repeat section B between sections A and C as shown in the diagram, right.*

1 Lay the back of the 20 cm x 46 cm piece of organza over the Lugana. Baste together 1 cm from the edge and overcast or overlock the edges.

2 Fold in half both ways and run a line of tacking down both folds. These lines of tacking form the centre guides for the embroidery.

3 Using the embroidery hoop to keep the fabrics taut and to stop them slipping against each other, begin the embroidery at the centre, working out towards the edges. Stitch all the satin stitch and kloster blocks in the pearl cotton.

4 Before sewing each eyelet, use the bodkin or stiletto to make a hole in the centre of each eyelet position. Take care not to break the threads, merely moving them apart. Use two strands of embroidery cotton for the eyelets.

5 Using doubled machine sewing thread, complete the beading.

CONSTRUCTION

❶ *All seam allowances of 1.5 cm are included in pattern pieces.*

1 Take one piece of organza for the ruched section. Leaving 2 cm at either end, run two gathering threads down each long side, one 10 mm from the edge and the other 20 mm from the edge. Gather up the material so that the piece measures 46 cm.

2 Lay the back of the gathered piece over the lining for the ruched section. Matching edges, stitch 12 mm from each edge. Overlock or overcast the edges.

3 Repeat for the second ruched section.

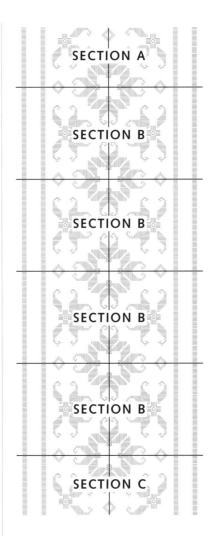

4 Stitch one ruched section to each side of the embroidered panel. Press seam allowances towards the centre panel.

5 Cut the piping cord into two 50 cm lengths. Lay the cord down the centre of one bias strip. Fold strip in half, enclosing the cord. Baste close to the cord to create the piping. Repeat with other bias strip and cord.

6 Lay piping over the edge of the front of the ruched section, matching edges. Baste. Repeat for the other end.

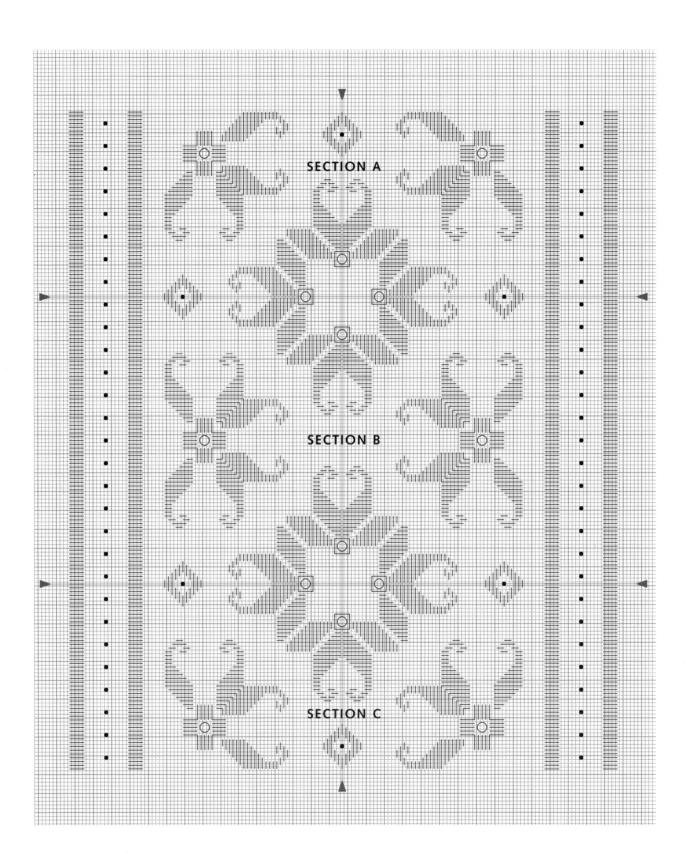

SECTION A

SECTION B

SECTION C

7 Overlock or overcast all the edges of the end sections of the organza.

8 Leaving 1.5 cm at each end, run two gathering threads down one long side of each end section, one 12 mm from the edge and the other 15 mm from the edge.

9 With right sides together, attach the ungathered edge of the end sections to the ruched panels. Use a zipper foot to stitch as close as possible to the piping.

10 With right sides together and seams matching, fold in half across all the panels to make a tube. From each end sew towards the centre, leaving a 29 cm opening for the zip.

11 Baste between the machine stitched sections. Press seam open. Pin zip in place, making sure it is centred. Using a small backstitch, hand sew the zip in place. Machine sew using a zipper foot if preferred.

12 Turn bolster cover out to the right side.

13 Tightly draw up gathering threads on end sections. Push finished edge inside through the centre of the gathering. Tie off gathering threads from the inside. Attach one button over the centre of the gathered section at each end.

14 Remove gathering threads from the ruched sections and all basting.

CUSHION INSERT CONSTRUCTION

1 Fold the square piece of lining in half to make a tube. Stitch along the long side, leaving a 10 cm opening in the centre of the seam.

2 Pin the circles to the ends of the tube, easing to fit. Stitch, clip seams and turn right side out.

3 Fill insert with polyester filling and whip stitch the opening closed.

4 Insert into bolster cover and close zip.

Index

Page numbers in **bold** refer to colour photographs.

ACKNOWLEDGMENTS

The author would like to thank all who have assisted in the formation of this book:

John Stanton; Julie Stanton; Brigitta Doyle; Frank and Yvonne Wilkey; Stephen Wilkey; Prue and Tim Scott; Joan Stanton; Jocelyn, Louise and Dianne at Hornsby Wool and Craft Nook; Catriona and Fiona at Material World, Hornsby; Margaret Fisher at The Crewel Gobelin, Killara; Barbara Reichert; Kate Finnie; Rosalyn Watnemo and Susan Meier, Nordic Needle, North Dakota USA; Mark and Karen Stanton; Ann Dale; Claire and Andrew Yule; Kim and Simon Gordon

and God, from whom all creativity flows.

The following sources are acknowledged as being helpful during the writing of this book.

Hardanger Basics and Beyond, Janice Love, Love and Stitches, 1990

Hardanger Embroidery, Jill Carter, Quilters' Resource Inc, 2000

Hardanger Fundamentals Made Fancy, Janice Love, Love and Stitches, 1993

Teach Yourself Hardanger Embroidery, Adelaide Stockdale, Leisure Arts, 1984

Traditional Hardanger Embroidery, The Priscilla Publishing Co, Dover Publications, 1985

www.nordicneedle.com

ABOUT THE AUTHOR

Yvette Stanton is an embroidery designer and book designer. In 2000 she won the Nordic Needle 22nd Annual Hardanger Embroidery Design Contest, based in North Dakota USA. She has also won many other prizes for her embroidery.

Yvette taught herself Hardanger embroidery while still at high school. She enjoys a wide range of embroidery styles and produces work for pleasure and on commission.

Yvette teaches embroidery and picture framing locally. Her embroidery is regularly featured in craft magazines.

Yvette Stanton lives in Sydney, Australia.

Chart symbols reference guide

Algerian eyelet stitch

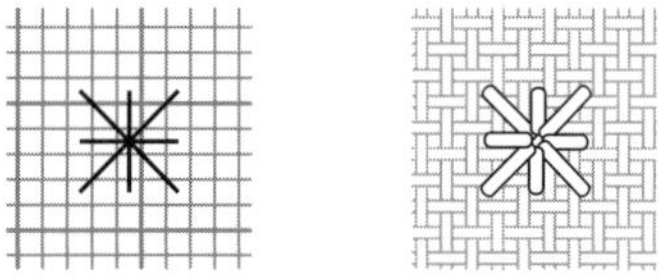

Beading

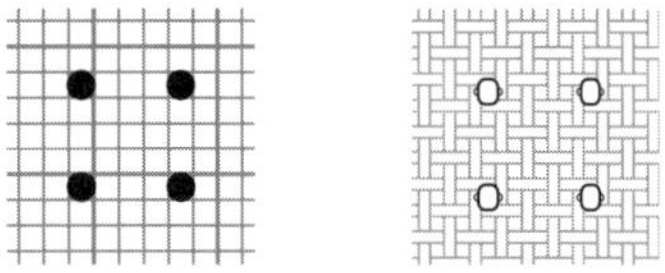

Buttonhole edge

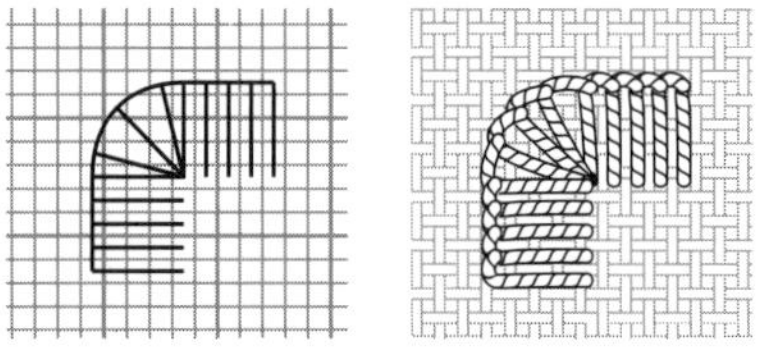

Cable stitch

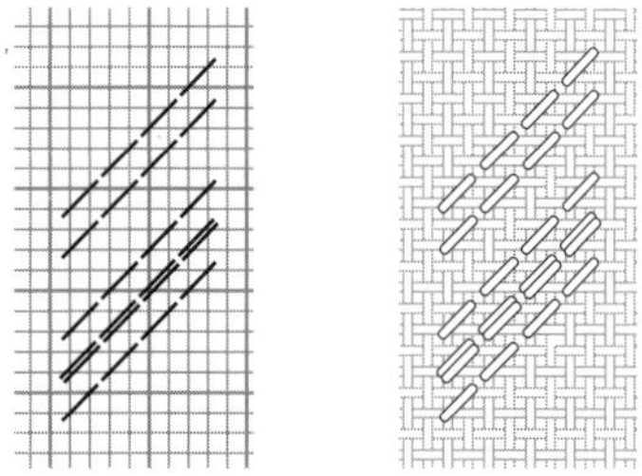

Dove's eye in a wrapped circle

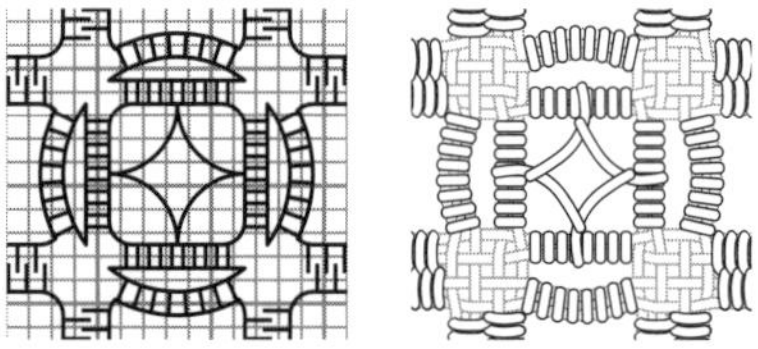

Dove's eye stitch

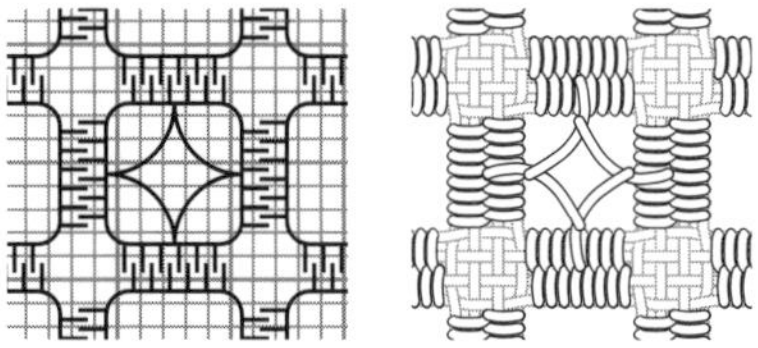

Eyelets

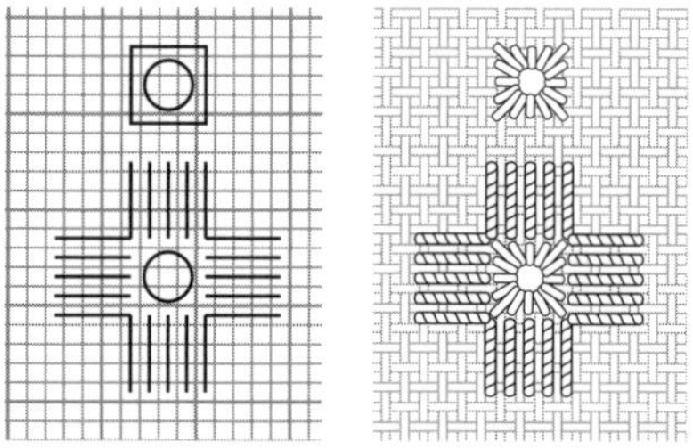

Faggot stitch

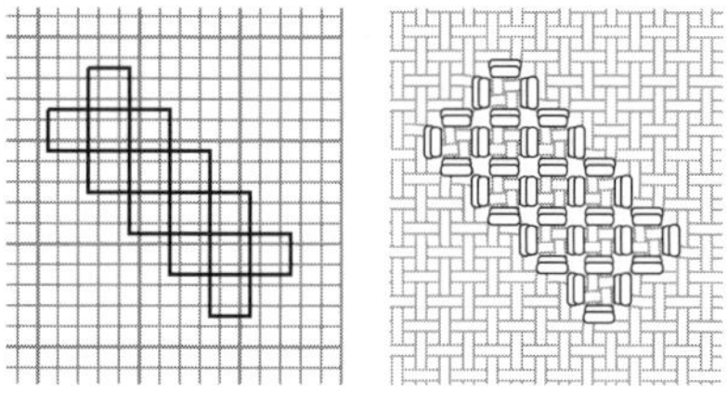

Four-sided stitch

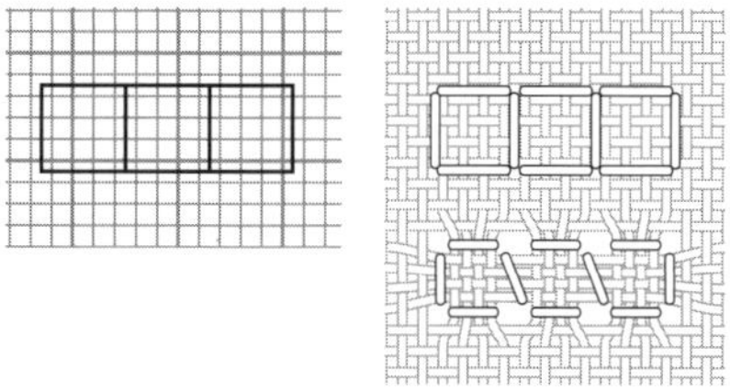

Greek cross

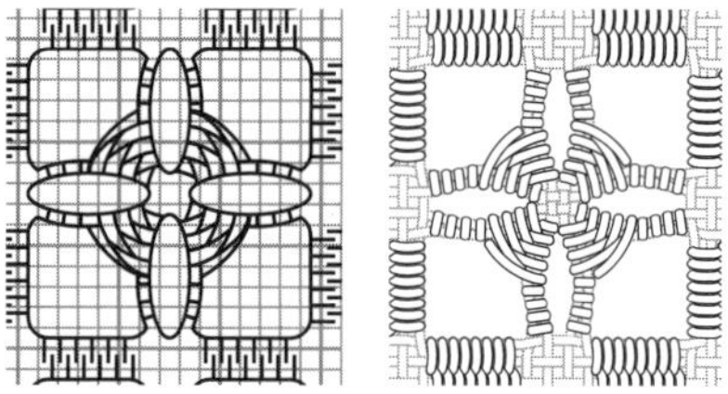

Greek cross border

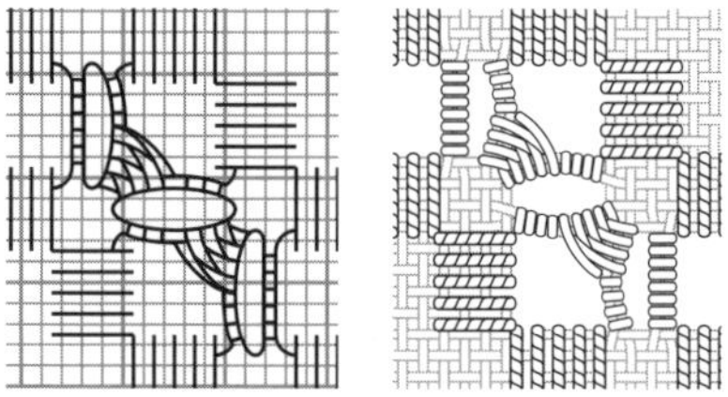

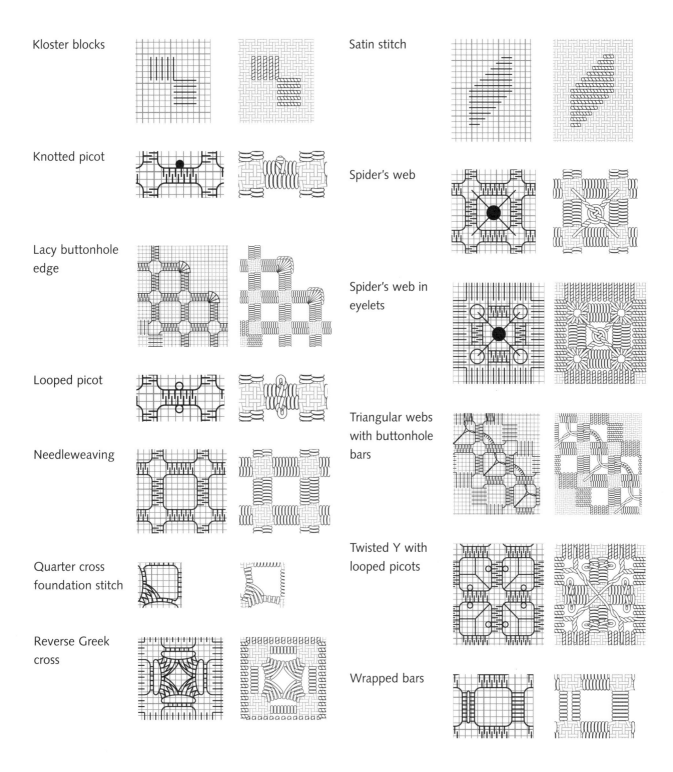

Kloster blocks

Knotted picot

Lacy buttonhole edge

Looped picot

Needleweaving

Quarter cross foundation stitch

Reverse Greek cross

Satin stitch

Spider's web

Spider's web in eyelets

Triangular webs with buttonhole bars

Twisted Y with looped picots

Wrapped bars

An Illustrated H

STOKE and NORTH STAFFORDSHIRE'S RAILWAYS

by
Allan C. Baker

IRWELL PRESS

For
Jack Hollick
Friend and Mentor

Cover photograph. Stoke station, looking south. The Fairburn Class 4 tank 42235 was a Stoke engine in the early 1950s – the shed never had many of the variety, but rather the Fowler and Stanier versions. Note 'Newcastle' bay to right. Two of the latter can be seen under the station roof. Note too, the youthful spotters on the No.2, Down, Platform.

Photograph back cover. Newfield Junction signal box in about 1960, one of the original Loop Line boxes. Despite the location of the wharf being at Newfields, the NSR always referred to it as Newfield - hence the name of the signal box. (Author's Collection)

First published in the United Kingdom in 2000
by Irwell Press
59A, High Street, Clophill,
Bedfordshire MK45 4BE

Contents

North Rode Junction on 30 September 1959, looking south and showing the junction and signal box. The train is the 8.0pm Colne to Euston, with Jubilee 45644 HOWE of Longsight shed. At this point the train would be building up speed on the 1 in 176 downgrade from Macclesfield Moss towards Congleton and Kidsgrove. The climb from Macclesfield to the Moss was almost two miles at 1 in 102 and trains were often banked out of Macclesfield. (Michael Mensing)

PREFACE

As one born and bred in North Staffordshire, and more particularly Stoke-on-Trent, I have said in a number of previous writings that my interest in the locality 'knows no bounds'. Despite having lived elsewhere for almost 25 years, I maintain a close interest in much that goes on there, and a lot of my research and writings concentrate on it. I was born into a family where a close interest in engineering and railways was second nature and so it was almost a foregone conclusion that railways would become my life. In 1962, therefore, I entered the service of the then London Midland Region of British Railways as a Motive Power Apprentice Fitter at Crewe North Shed. Henceforth, I travelled on the lines of the former North Staffordshire Railway almost daily, from my 'home' station of Etruria, to Crewe. I did, however, spend some time at Cockshute Diesel Rail Car Depot at Cliff Vale, and the odd brief stint at Stoke steam shed.

During my schoolboy days trainspotting was a regular pastime, usually at either Etruria, ten minutes from home or, once I became more mobile on a push bike, further afield at Cockshute or Stoke itself. Summer evenings after school would generally find me somewhere near a railway line, and at weekends I would often go further afield to Stableford, Whitmore or Madeley to get more variety on the West Coast main line. Trips by train, originally with Dad on Saturday mornings to Crewe and later on my own to Derby, followed. As time went on I ventured further afield, to Wolverhampton, for example, to see those nice green engines with copper capped chimneys! I took notes from an early age, and still retain a collection of notebooks and Ian Allan ABCs, together with timetables – which fascinated me – leaflets and the like. Through the local Model Engineering Society (father was a keen and extremely accomplished model engineer, with numerous 3½ and 5in. gauge working scale models to his credit) we knew several Stoke footplatemen. Later, via the Society, we got to know Geoff Sands, a great enthusiast, when he arrived at Stoke as Shed Master, from far away Melton Constable. Thus, we were in receipt of much 'official' information, the occasional footplate ride and other perquisites.

Stoke's locomotives were, unfortunately, rather a mundane lot, consisting in the main of ex-LMS standard types; 3F 0-6-0Ts, 4F 0-6-0 tender engines, 'Crab' 2-6-0s, Fowler and Stanier 4MT 2-6-4Ts and a few Stanier Class 5s. Their work was made up largely of local passenger trains for which the tanks abounded, and coal and other mineral traffic to the area's numerous collieries, iron and steel works and engineering concerns. Strangely, little of the products for which the locality is so justly famous – china and earthenware – were transported by rail at the time I write of, and none of the Potteries ('Pot Banks' in local parlance) sported enough siding space or traffic to justify their own locomotive. Hence the highlight of any day's spotting hereabouts were the Manchester-London trains, several of which were routed via Macclesfield and Stoke to rejoin the West Coast Main Line at Colwich, south of Stafford, or vice versa. These were the preserve of Longsight and Camden shed, the former using its Britannia Pacifics on these double home jobs. I recall with affection 70031 BYRON, 70032 TENNYSON and 70033 CHARLES DICKENS, Longsight steeds for many a year and almost exclusive motive power on the 2.05pm Manchester to London train, due away from Stoke at 3.15pm. Without checking my notebooks, I cannot recall ever seeing this train without one of these three in charge, until the diesels arrived!

Despite the lack of 'namers', many of Stoke's regulars became firm friends; indeed, they had been on the local allocation year after year. One remembers 4F 0-6-0 'Standard Freights' ('Stoke Scots' to the local enginemen) 44308-44310, 44499 and 44502, 3F 0-6-0Ts 47496, 47499, 47609 and 47610, Class 4 2-6-4Ts 42364, 42375, 42543, 42567, 42603, 42609 and 42670 to recall but a few. My notebooks record sighting these regulars time and time again.

The North Staffordshire Railway was legendary in the running powers it exercised, far in excess of the total route mileage of its own system, and this tradition continued well after the old company ceased to exist. Stoke men could be found all the year round at places as far afield as Leeds, Wellingborough and London among many others and during the summer at Llandudno, Blackpool and Liverpool – for the Isle of Man steamers. They were also legendary for the distances they would go both with their own engines, and tender first; indeed, they were a standing joke with many of their contemporaries all over the London Midland system, for their willingness to make lengthy runs in this uncomfortable fashion.

During the traditional 'Stoke Wakes' fortnight (the Potteries adopted the northern manufacturing town philosophy of a two-week annual shutdown, under the appellation of 'Wakes') the supply of 'Crabs' and Class 5s would soon be exhausted on the numerous specials run to and from the popular destinations for the Pottery folk. Of course, engines would be borrowed from nearby sheds, with Crewe North and South providing most, but even these were exhaustible, and Stoke men would think nothing of heading for Blackpool or Llandudno with a 4F and, if necessary, tender first! For a week or so before the annual exodus commenced – it was always the first two weeks in August – trains of empty coaching stock would start to arrive, to be stabled in all sorts of places normally the preserve of lesser vehicles. Pratts Sidings at Stoke would soon fill up, rakes would be found at Etruria, Cresswell, Newchapel and Goldenhill on the Loop Line, Alsager, Longport and other places. The goods-only lines along the Biddulph Valley, and to Leek, which had long lost their passenger services (as far back as 1927 in the former case) would all of a sudden see a re-opening of long-slumbering stations, and special trains would call. Stoke station would become a hive of activity and the timetabling and diagramming of all the specials, intermingled with the normal traffic, was a sight to see. Trains would appear from all the branches, usually with smaller engines, to exchange them for larger ones, often with combined trains, for the onward journeys. The steep gradients of the Loop Line were a particular problem, and to see ten, eleven and even twelve coach trains worked over this curving, undulating route, usually by a brace of Class 4 tanks, and having to draw up at stations with short platforms two and sometimes three times, was a thing never to be a forgotten. Whatever derogatory remarks were expressed about Stoke footplatemen by those from elsewhere, their enginemanship was second to none. Indeed, in their daily lot, working the numerous loose coupled, unbraked mineral trains, not only over the Loop, but on other sharply graded, winding and twisting lines around the area, called for enginemanship of the highest standard – and the goods guards had to be good too!

Through membership of the local Model Engineering Society, and the North Staffordshire & Cheshire Traction Engine Club, Dad and I made the acquaintance of the late Dr J.R. Hollick, of 'Manifold' fame. Jack regularly came along to meetings to talk so enthusiastically and authoritatively about the old North Stafford. I well remember years earlier, Dad borrowing a copy of the unequalled 'Manifold' history of the North Stafford, and we studied it together over and over again, before that is, we were able to own our own copy. Jack befriended me from this tender age, when I had nothing to offer in return for his fund of knowledge and material. However, an interest in those small locomotives one saw in and around collieries, iron and steel works, and other similar sites, and which had names and not numbers, and were not in the Ian Allan ABC, fascinated me. It was an expanding knowledge of these, earned through visiting the locations and by membership of the Birmingham Locomotive Club, Industrial Locomotives Information Section (later the Industrial Railway Society), that enabled me to feed a little back to Jack in return - for he too, shared a love for this lesser brethren of the locomotive world.

More mobile, with school friend Alan Martin, we explored lesser used lines on our bikes, and I vividly recall cycling alongside the track of much of the Audley line, Trentham Park branch, the track beds of the Apedale-Podmore Hall Mineral Railway, the Talk branch and others – oh! for a camera. When a car (actually Mother's Austin A35 van) and camera eventually came along I made it my business to photograph much of what I explored, and some of the better of my efforts illustrate the pages that follow. A particular interest in signalling made me pay special attention to signal boxes, and among my most prized artefacts are a pair of NSR Tyer's single wire, three position block instruments. I have the Down line instrument from Brampton Sidings to Apedale Junction, and the Up line instrument from Burslem to Cobridge – as a pair, they can, and have worked together, albeit only in my home. They are beautiful pieces of Victorian signal engineering. Making friends with several local Signalmen, I learnt something of the art of mechanical signalling.

Readers will appreciate from the foregoing that compiling this book has been a richly nostalgic experience. I have tried to recapture the air of the old North Stafford in my time, but I have also interspersed this with something of the NSR itself, and the great and mighty LMS. When I started my railway career, there were many men still at work who had begun with the pre-grouping companies, and even more with the LMS. Being at Crewe, most of my experiences with pre-grouping men concerned those who had worked for the London & North Western, but I did work alongside a few from the 'Knotty', and lots who recalled with much affection that old company's engines. The NSR bequeathed the most modern and well maintained fleet of locomotives to the LMS, far outweighing any of its contemporaries in their advanced development, size for size. As the late E.S. Cox has stated, it was only the mindless quest of Midlandisation that prevented one at least (the new L 0-6-2T) from becoming an early LMS standard, rather than the perpetuation of much inferior and older Midland designs, as an interim measure between the locomotive management regimes of Fowler and Stanier. As it was, the quest for standardisation reduced this modern NSR fleet of soundly designed, easy to maintain, robust and much-loved locomotives to the scrap heap in record time. A brace of Class 'M' 0-4-4 tanks, dating from 1908 and 1920, were the last to go, in 1939.

As time went on I witnessed the gradual replacement of the old Midland and LMS types, superseded by more modern British Railways Standard designs, of which Stoke accumulated large numbers. Then of course came the onslaught of the diesels, electrification of the main line and closure of the branch lines. The latter generally followed the reduction in local freight traffic, and the never-ending rounds of closures of the area's many collieries. Indeed, there was only one deep mine in the North Staffordshire coalfield by 1998, at Silverdale, which happily saw traffic over the then only remaining NSR branch line, albeit

but a truncated portion of the Market Drayton line, between Madeley and Silverdale. This too, closed in December 1998, and with it this remaining portion of the route.

There is, unfortunately, little left today. The heavy industry has largely disappeared, the colliery dirt tips have been landscaped, and the railway track beds have either been completely obliterated or have become walkways. It is often said that an interest in a district, and love of it, is enhanced when one moves to distant parts – things are no longer taken quite so much for granted. This is certainly so in my case, and in the period since I left the area as my professional career progressed, I have spent much time and effort in a study of its railway and industrial history. This has resulted in several books of which this is the latest, and while it is largely pictorial, I have tried to choose not only a representative selection of views, but also as many as possible that have not appeared in print before. I have also attempted to give informative captions, and other data, so that the book is something of a reference work, with a lot of facts not readily accessible elsewhere. Many of these are not so easy to find in any easily available reference book, but they are here for those willing to delve! One day, doubtless in retirement, I hope to devote time to studies of the Audley and Biddulph Valley lines, on a similar scale to my work on the Potteries Loop Line. Much of the research has been undertaken, but it awaits the time that a professional career just does not allow. I hope, therefore, to crave my reader's indulgence with this less weighty effort, yet one which (I hope) still serves a useful purpose, covering in photographs a period of railway history in North Staffordshire not hitherto encompassed by other writers. Principal among these are the valuable contributions of my old friend and NSR collaborator, Basil Jeuda. Basil's books have, hitherto, largely concentrated on the NSR period itself.

In conclusion, it only remains to thank those who have helped me in these efforts, all of whom I hope I have listed below. I hope too, they will forgive me doing no more than listing them like this, though I would, however, like to single out a particular few. For splendid support with photographs and proof reading (he was not only able to locate the odd slip of the pen, but also correct my memory on more than one occasion, and make me check a few facts too!) a very old friend, Mike Fell. Mike and I were together on joint explorations when many of the photographs that illustrate these pages were taken, and we regularly met on Sunday mornings to exchange notes, and study the results of each other's recent expeditions. Dave Donkin, a colleague for many years of my involvement with the preserved local Foxfield Railway, and a joint participant on several foreign trips, has put his entire collection of local photographs at my disposal. As will be seen, Dave was very active in and around Stoke itself in the latter days of steam. John Bucknall has helped me

On 26 September 1960 Class 4F No.44352 of Alsager shed emerges from the middle Harecastle Tunnel, with a southbound ballast train, doubtless for some relaying work on the following Sunday. From mid-LMS days Alsager's allocation was exclusively these engines, together with Class 3F shunting tanks. (Michael Mensing)

in the Stafford area, Michael Mensing has again been extremely helpful, as has my old friend, Tim Shuttleworth. Tim's excellent printing skills have brought much out of some pretty lousy negatives, indeed results never thought possible before! Basil Jeuda, I have already mentioned; last but by no means least, I must thank Robert Keys, for putting up with my continual bombardment of queries, and who has as a consequence, delved deeply into his large collection of NSR material, and at times when this was not really convenient.

My long-standing friend and mentor, the late Dr J.R. (Jack) Hollick, features large in anything and everything I write in connection with the area. Jack and I corresponded almost continuously from the early 1960s, until his untimely death in 1991. He passed on to me much information, photographs and the like; indeed Jack was always willing to share his fund of knowledge and collection of material, not only with me, but anyone with a genuine interest in the North Stafford. After his death, I was glad to have been able to catalogue his collection on behalf of the Foxfield Light Railway So-

ciety, to which body he donated it, prior to depositing the collection in Hanley Reference Library, on loan from the Society. There it can be made available for all to see, as Jack so much wanted. Thank you Jack, for everything, and I hope you would have approved of this latest effort on the railways of North Staffordshire, which you loved so much.

My mother and father, mother still living in retirement in the area, were extremely supportive of my hobby, and 'Dad' is largely responsible for fostering and encouraging my interest from an early age. We did much together in those early, formative years. Last, but by no means least, Angela and Kevin who continue to put up with hours of 'Dad' located away in his study, during what are already extremely limited periods of spare time. To them all, a big, big thank you, along with
Bernard Holland
Martin Connop-Price
J W P Rowledge
Clive Guthrie
Allen Civil
William Jack

Over the years extensive use was made of excellent facilities at the following depositories of information: The Public Record Office, Hanley Reference Library, Keele University Reference Library, Staffordshire County Record Office, House of Lords Record Office.

Useful books include the pioneer work by 'Manifold', *The North Staffordshire Railway*, published in 1952 by J.H. Henstock of Ashbourne, and much sought-after today on the second-hand market. Its authors were Jack Hollick, Claude Moreton, Nowell Nowell-Gossling, Mike Page and Bill Stubbs, of whom Jack and Mike are no longer with us. Rex Christiansen and Bob Miller's *The North Staffordshire Railway*, published by David & Charles in 1971, has also proved very useful. Then there are the writings of my valued friend Basil Jeuda, including his *Railways of The Macclesfield District* (Wyvern Publications 1984), *The Macclesfield, Bollington & Marple Railway* (Cheshire County Council 1983), *The Railways Of Macclesfield* (Foxline 1995), *The Leek, Caldon & Waterhouses Railway* (North Staffordshire Railway Company (1978)

and *The Knotty* (Lightmoor Press 1996). There are also my own books which include *The Potteries Loop Line* (Trent Valley Publications 1986), *The Cheadle Railway* (Oakwood Press 1979), *The Cheadle Collieries & Their Railways* (Trent Valley Publications 1986) and *The Industrial Locomotives of North Staffordshire* (Industrial Railway Society 1997). Most if not all these books are now out of print but they are, nevertheless, recommended reading for those who would like to find out more of the fascinating history of this wonderful part of our country. Interest in the area seems to know no bounds, and a small library of books have appeared over the last few years, from a number of authors. But as I have already said, this one, I hope, addresses areas and issues not hitherto dealt with in such detail – largely the period of BR ownership since nationalisation, and in the main covering the days of steam.

Allan C Baker,
Highfield House,
High Halden,
Kent,
April 1999

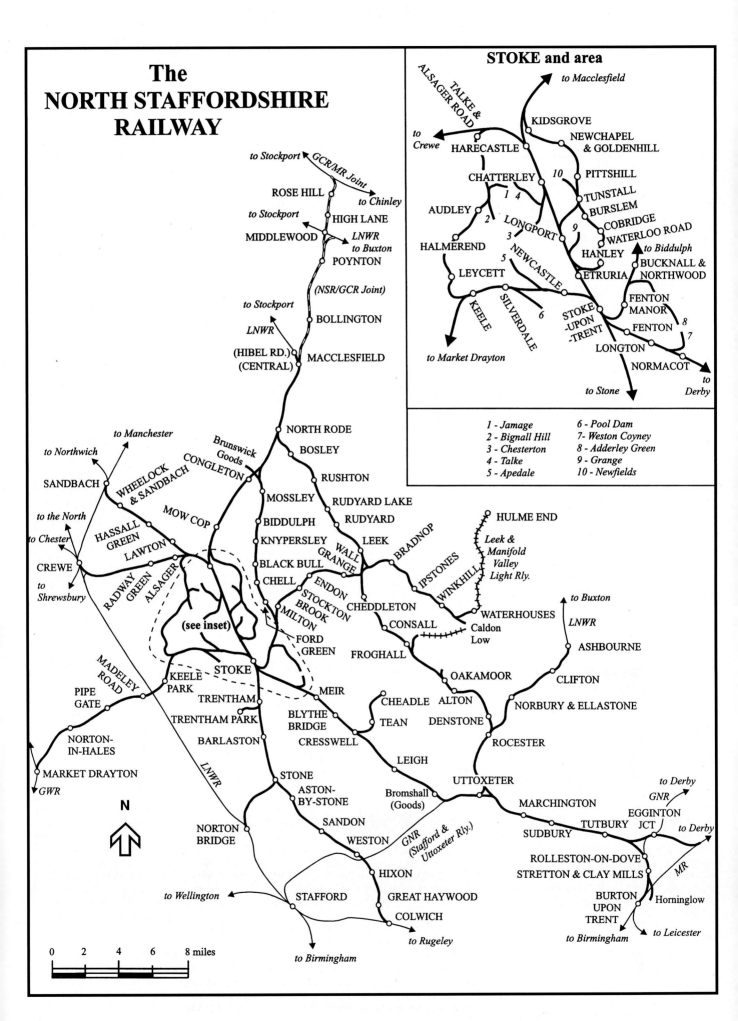

The NORTH STAFFORDSHIRE RAILWAY

STOKE and area

Key to inset:
1 - Jamage
2 - Bignall Hill
3 - Chesterton
4 - Talke
5 - Apedale
6 - Pool Dam
7 - Weston Coyney
8 - Adderley Green
9 - Grange
10 - Newfields

0 2 4 6 8 miles

N

Introduction

Public railways arrived in the north of Staffordshire with the opening of the first lines of the North Staffordshire Railway, in 1848. This company was born out of local pressure groups failing to convince the promoters of the Manchester & Birmingham Railway to build their line through the area. There had been plans (in 1837) for this railway to pass through the Potteries by way of the Chatterley Valley, and surveys were undertaken to this end. One of the reasons for its failure to come to fruition were the gradients necessary to climb over Harecastle Hill at Kidsgrove, an obstacle eventually circumvented by the North Staffordshire Railway, boring a series of tunnels.

There was another, practical, reason for avoiding North Staffordshire; by the time the Manchester & Birmingham Railway got around to building its line, the Grand Junction Railway was making its own line northwards from Stafford, west of the Potteries, to what became Crewe. Clearly then, it was easier for the Manchester & Birmingham to go by way of Cheadle Hulme and Sandbach, to join the Grand Junction at Crewe. The story is a little more complicated than this, because it was the good worthies of the loyal and ancient Borough of New-castle-under-Lyme, which lies west of the Pottery towns, who had earlier campaigned to keep the Grand Junction away from their boundaries. Thus, in the event, it passed on the fringe of the county, some five miles to the west. Such was the opposition to railways in some quarters in those days, and here we had two adjacent municipalities, one for, and one against the encroachment of the new railway.

The NSR, colloquially known as the 'Knotty' by virtue of its Staffordshire Knot insignia, came to dominate the area, perhaps to a greater extent than any other of the smaller pre-grouping railways elsewhere in the country. North Staffordshire is an extremely distinct part of this large county, with a culture and people as different from the southern end as could be envisaged. There are absolutely no ties with Wolverhampton and the Black Country – for which Staffordshire is perhaps better known – in any way, shape or form. It really has no ties with *anywhere* else, though within but a few miles it has borders with Shropshire to the west, Derbyshire to the east and Cheshire to the north. It is justly famous the world over for its china and earthenware, the result of a thriving pottery manufacturing industry that developed following the discovery of the clays, marl and coal that abounded in the locality. Inland transport therefore came early to the area, with a number of notable businessmen of the pottery industry anxious to get their wares to the export markets via the River Mersey at Liverpool and Birkenhead, and via the River Trent, and thence the Humber. Thus this country's first trunk canal came about in 1777, the Grand Trunk – later The Trent & Mersey – which opened throughout from Preston Brook in the north to Shardlow in the south and thus joined the two great rivers of the Mersey and the Trent. James Brindley was of course the Engineer, and perhaps the most famous potter of all time, Josiah Wedgwood, was extremely prominent in its promotion. Wedgwood built his manufactory alongside the route of the canal, together with a village to house his workers, at what became Etruria, north of Stoke town itself. This famous village, today but a shadow of its former self, took its name from the ancient Etruscans, whose work Wedgwood tried so hard, and largely successfully, to emulate in his pottery wares.

From its centre in Stoke-upon-Trent, the NSR penetrated in all directions, and it fought long and hard to keep other railways out of its domain. In this it was

Beautiful Alton Towers, 19 Aug 1961, with the 11.25am Leek-Uttoxeter hauled by Stoke's 2-6-4T No.42323. Notice the unusual design of signal box, situated on the platform. After the Earls of Shrewsbury moved, Alton Towers became a well known and popular pleasure resort, hence the change of name of the station. It was always a popular destination for excursions right up until the line finally closed south of Oakamoor. The workman's passenger services ceased on 4 January 1965 and the section of line south of Oakamoor closed on the same day. (Michael Mensing)

perhaps, more successful than any of the pre-grouping companies. In its early days it fought manfully and consistently to keep its mighty neighbour the London & North Western (an amalgam of 1846, of the Grand Junction, Manchester & Birmingham, London & Birmingham and other railways) at bay both in and out of Parliament. But the plucky North Stafford survived it all, and not for nothing was it described as the 'Little Octopus', as its tentacles struck out in all directions to preserve the locality upon which it had laid its claim. Battles were also fought on its western frontier against the Great Western, again both in and out of Parliament, as various GW-backed schemes attempted to gain access from that direction. This particular campaign resulted in a number of compromises agreed in Parliamentary Select Committees, and the NSR was forced to build a number of lines it might otherwise not have bothered with. In some of these cases it showed its disregard in the dilatory way it subsequently went about the task of construction.

Coming to terms with the LNWR meant that running powers – and extensive ones at that – were conceded over each other's lines, and thereafter the two companies, the giant and the relative pigmy, worked together in perfect harmony. Indeed, the LNWR frequently helped out its much, much, smaller neighbour, and in any number of ways,

rather in the spirit of an uncle and nephew relationship. Never can so large a railway company have been so benevolent to so small a neighbour, and the two worked together thus for the remainder of their independent days. One of the most prominent manifestations of this was the running of a proportion of the through London to Manchester traffic over the NSR between Colwich or Norton Bridge and Macclesfield, with North Stafford engines working the trains from Manchester London Road to Stoke, where the North Western engines took over.

At the Grouping in 1923 the NSR made contact with the LNWR at no less than six places (seven if the LNWR sidings and yard, deep in MR territory at Burton-on-Trent are included). There were two connections with the Midland, another at the GWR and two more at the Great Northern. These last two GNR connections were in effect the same line, with the junction at Eggington, and then the Stafford & Uttoxeter line onwards from Bromshall Junction – the GNR enjoying running powers between the two. Moreover, like the LNWR, the Great Northern had a yard and sidings at Burton-on-Trent, so if this is included, there was yet another connection between these two railways. The NSR had also (with the Great Central Railway) been joint owner of the Macclesfield, Bollington and Marple Railway. Such was

the extent of its running powers over neighbouring systems that the NSR worked greater distances over 'foreign' railways than over its own, and its engines and men were regularly shedded at outposts far from the parent system. Never to be outdone, it held its head high among contemporaries and despite its small size became a constituent of the newly formed London Midland & Scottish Railway at the 1923 Grouping, rather than suffer the lot of the other railways of similar size, which merely became 'absorbed companies'. In this way it qualified for its own Directorial appointment to the newly formed Board of the LMS, then the largest Joint Stock Company operating a railway anywhere in the world. It was indeed, in what it had achieved, and how it achieved it, a formidable little railway.

The area served by the NSR was not just dominated by the Potteries and ancillary industries, but also by large scale mining of minerals, discovered in the quest for the clay and marl. There were extensive coal and ironstone workings, and a thriving iron, and later steel industry, was born, along with heavy engineering. Not only did the NSR build the majority of its own locomotives, at Stoke, but there were other locomotive, carriage and wagon builders in the area too. Much of the railway's traffic was in connection with these industries, and lines were developed to serve their needs. Some

Kidsgrove Liverpool Road on 26 September 1960, with the Up Radway Green workers' train about to leave for its trip over the Loop Line. This train ran in both directions, to take workers to and from the Pottery towns to the ROF Factory at Radway Green and was the remnant of much more extensive workings of the War years. It started at Crewe at 4.26pm and after running empty to Radway Green, ran all stations to Cresswell with a reversal at Kidsgrove to gain access to the Loop. It did the reverse in the morning, running empty from Radway Green to Crewe, where the stock was stabled during the day. The engine here is a Stoke Class 4 tank, No.42668; notice Kidsgrove Liverpool Road Junction signal box in the left distance. Special provision was made in the Sectional Appendix for the propelling of passenger trains between Kidsgrove Central Junction and the Loop Line Junction. This train, which continued to run for a number of years afterwards, was not advertised in the public timetables. Those of us in the know used it however, including the section from Radway Green to Crewe, when it suited our personal movements! Latterly, it was routed via the main line rather than the Loop. (Michael Mensing)

The famous 'Tutbury Jenny' push-pull working propelling away from Tutbury for Burton-on-Trent with ex-Midland Railway 0-4-4T No.58080 (ex-LMS No.1411, built 1900) on 20 September 1952. This was the nickname for the Burton to Tutbury local service, always the preserve of an engine from Burton NSR shed; when this closed after the grouping the task passed to ex-Midland and LNWR engines from the other sheds. Until closed on 1 January 1949, these workings also served Horninglow, Stretton & Clay Mills and Rolleston-on-Dove. Latterly, motive power was either an Ivatt Class 2 2-6-2T or the BR Standard 84XXX equivalent, with Ivatt 41277 working the service on the last day, 11 June 1960. (FW Shuttleworth)

lines, as a consequence, never boasted passenger services.

The general state of the economy in the country after the First World War was poor, and dealt with North Staffordshire as badly as most other industrial areas. Closures of collieries, iron and steel works and other engineering establishments came quick and heavy. The LMS wasted no time in coming to terms with this, and the size of the former NSR network was reduced to suit. Passenger services suffered quickly, and extensively: 'The Plunder of The North Staffordshire', as Robert Keys so aptly put it, in his October 1956 *Trains Illustrated* article. The system at Grouping consisted of just over 156 miles of double track route, and all but sixty miles of single track – including the 2ft.6in. gauge Leek & Manifold Valley Light Railway. There was also the twelve mile double track stretch of the Macclesfield, Bollington & Marple Railway, jointly owned with the Great Central.

The first closure came in July 1927, when passenger services were withdrawn from the line between Milton Junction and Congleton, consisting as it did of much of the Biddulph Valley line. Three years later it was the turn of the Sandbach line to lose its passenger services, followed in April 1931 by the Audley line. And so it went on, continuing unabated by British Railways after Nationalisation in January 1948. So, by the late 1960s, only the Churnet Valley line, the Market Drayton line as far as Silverdale, the Loop Line and Cheadle branch survived with a passenger service, and very

sparse it was too, in many cases. The Churnet went, to all intents and purposes, in November 1960, the Cheadle branch in June 1963, and the remainder in March 1964. The former joint line, the Macclesfield Bollington & Marple, closed in January 1970.

The NSR engines did not fare much better, with the first withdrawals coming in 1925. Thereafter it was a rapid slaughter, so much so that from a Grouping total of 196 locomotives, there were but 99 left in 1931 and 36 in 1935. By 1939 there were no more in main line service and only a handful (new L Class 0-6-2Ts in the main) remained in industrial service – though a battery electric locomotive was retained for shunting at Oakamoor. This came about despite a large proportion of the NSR fleet being modern, powerful and superheated tank engines, acclaimed by such a notable engineer as the late E.S. Cox, as among the best in the country. The North Stafford, with its many branch lines and sharp curves, was always very much a tank engine railway and as a consequence extensive bunker first running was the order of the day. Passenger tender engines were, by and large, confined to Crewe to Derby trains – the longest regular through passenger workings on the system – but they also found use on the summer through workings to Llandudno, as well as other excursions. As yet another example of the co-operation between the LNWR and the North Stafford, although there were no 'formal' running powers granted to the smaller company over the North Wales line, its engines, men and

rolling stock worked regular timetabled services in the summer months to and from Llandudno – a favourite holiday haunt for Potteries folk. The majority of the goods tender engines were used on the main line, especially those goods trains running off the system.

After the 1923 Grouping of course, there was an influx of ex-LNWR and Midland types, as was to be expected with their much larger numbers – despite, in some cases, inferior performance. Ex-LNWR 'Georges' and 'Precursors' became regulars on the through Manchester to Birmingham workings that were soon introduced, and some of these trains went via the Loop Line. In 1926 Stoke received the first of the 4F 0-6-0s, (a Midland design perpetuated as an LMS standard), and members of this class remained on the shed's allocation until as late as 1965. The Fowler, and later Stanier Class 4 2-6-4Ts started to arrive in 1929, displacing more of the indigenous engines on local passenger workings. Eventually Stoke had more of the Stanier engines on its allocation than any other shed on the LMS, a total of no less than 34. They eventually had almost exclusive control of the local passenger jobs and together with ten of the Fowler variety made up the complement of 2-6-4Ts on the eve of nationalisation in December 1947. Some of these individual engines, and the 4Fs, remained at Stoke shed for over 25 years.

As well as Stoke, the NSR had engine sheds at Alsager, Macclesfield, Uttoxeter, Ashbourne, Colwich, Crewe, Derby, Burton-on-Trent, Leek and Market

Drayton – albeit not all at the same time. They were quite small affairs compared with Stoke, and Colwich was an early casualty, closing in 1896. There is also believed to have been one at Norton Bridge in the early days. Several closed soon after grouping, at places where the larger companies already had sheds, as would be expected. Crewe went on 30 March 1923, and Burton and Derby on 30 June 1923. Leek had been replaced by a new shed at Leek Brook in late 1905, in connection with opening of the line to Waterhouses and Caldon and it closed in its turn on 4 January 1932. Ashbourne closed November 1932, engines thereafter running light to and from Uttoxeter as necessary while Market Drayton, which dated from 1873, and occupied part of the former Great Western premises there, closed on 8 December 1934. This left only Alsager, Uttoxeter and Macclesfield to pass into BR ownership; the first closed on 18 June 1962, Macclesfield 12 June 1961, and Uttoxeter 7 December 1964. In LMS and BR days the ex-NSR sheds came within the Crewe District, with the exception of Macclesfield, which was under the jurisdiction of Manchester Longsight. Latterly, under the LMS system, they were coded: Stoke 5D, Alsager 5F, Uttoxeter 5E, Macclesfield 9C. Uttoxeter was to all intents and purposes a sub-shed, or 'outstation' of Stoke; likewise Alsager was sub to Crewe South, and Macclesfied a sub-shed of Longsight.

In BR days the allocation at Stoke consisted largely of the 2-6-4Ts and 4F 0-6-0s whose arrival was chronicled above. As well as these, there were 3F shunting tanks, and a few other odd types, as well as a small band of Class 5 4-6-0s. These were used on the long distance fitted freights, and Stoke men had regular nightly 'double home' jobs (that is, lodging turns) to Camden and Leeds. At weekends these engines would be in demand for excursions, but Stoke would consistently borrow locomotives during the summer months for such work, generally from Crewe North and Crewe South. Later these classes were joined by Stanier Class 6P/5F 2-6-0s, and some Hughes/Fowler 'Crabs', but until the early 1960s, Stoke was really the preserve of the 2-6-4Ts and the 4F 'Standard Freights'.

The Crewe to Derby passenger workings were generally Crewe North and Derby diagrams, and brought Ivatt Class 4 2-6-0s from Derby and Black Fives from Crewe North, and there were numerous regular visitors from other sheds on goods and mineral workings. The ex-LNWR 'Super D' 0-8-0s were always to be seen, along with Stanier and 'Austerity' 8F 2-8-0s. The Manchester to London expresses were the preserve of Longsight and Camden sheds, largely the former, with Jubilees, Royal Scot 4-6-0s and the Longsight Britannias predominating.

The first services to be dieselised in the area were those from Crewe to Derby, initially with railcar sets operated and maintained from Crewe, beginning with the winter timetable of 16 September 1957. The units were those built by the Birmingham Railway Carriage & Wagon Co. Ltd. of Smethwick, (BRCW), three-car sets with two driving powered vehi-

The grand frontage to Stoke station.

cles and a trailer in the middle. These later became Class 104 in the BR classification scheme. In anticipation of extension of diesel services onto the Manchester to Birmingham jobs, together with the remaining locals, a new maintenance depot for the railcars was built at Cockshute Sidings, Cliffe Vale. This was north of Stoke, where the Market Drayton line left the main line at Newcastle Junction, and was already used for carriage maintenance and servicing. Construction started in early 1957, the building being 454ft. long with three roads, each capable of holding two three car sets, six sets in all. Facilities were on three levels, with the pitted roads supported on stilts, to give better access to underframe equipment. For part of the shed's length there were solebar height platforms, to assist in body maintenance and cleaning. The depot opened in October 1957, and the Manchester to Birmingham trains and the local services went over to diesel traction on 3 March 1958. Cockshute had an allocation of 35 three-car BRCW sets, and three two-car

sets (also BRCW) together with a solitary Cravens single car parcels unit; it also took over maintenance of the diesel shunters when they arrived in the area a year or so later. Once this new facility, and one at Derby Etches Park opened, maintenance of the sets at Crewe ceased, allowing the men and equipment there to be concentrated on the diesel main line locomotives then beginning to appear. Once all the sets were in use steam haulage on local passenger trains almost ceased, but there were a few odd workings, largely special workmen's trains. Examples were the Radway Green ROF factory workers' train, the staff train to and from Crewe Works (a legacy of the closure of Stoke Works by the LMS in 1926, when most of the men transferred to Crewe), and Wedgwood's Pottery Works trains at Barlaston. Of course, steam reigned supreme for a few more years on seasonal main line trains to holiday destinations, excursions and the like.

Unfortunately, the new arrangements at Cockshute were to be short-lived, and indeed it was outlasted by the steam shed at Stoke! Under the London Midland Region electrification plans the line from Cheadle Hulme via Macclesfield to Norton Bridge and Colwich was to be electrified at 25KV, and this spelled the doom for Cockshute. The Manchester to Birmingham services were to go over to electric traction and as we have already seen, the local branch lines were closing. There was more than enough capacity at Derby to maintain the sets working the Crewe to Derby services, and any other workings around Crewe could be serviced at Chester. The overhead line equipment was brought into use in the area on October 3 1966, the Harecastle Tunnel Diversion scheme having opened on the 27 June. The power signal box at Stoke was commissioned on 18 July, replacing fourteen old mechanical boxes and controlled fifteen route miles and 34½ track miles; about the same time, new semi-mechanical boxes were commissioned at Kidsgrove Central Junction and Grange Junction. Some electric working commenced in January 1967, still on diesel timings, but it was 6 March before full electric working began. This included not only the Manchester to Birmingham services, but also the through London to Manchester trains that were routed this way, Stoke in fact getting a better service from these trains than it ever had hitherto. As a prelude to this, Cockshute Depot ended its short life, and closed on 6 March 1966. The building nevertheless remained in use for a while, for the diesel locomotives working in the area, but soon the fuelling facilities were withdrawn, with the locomotives largely supplied from Crewe. It closed completely in the late 1970s, and has since been sold and converted for industrial use.

Stoke shed acquired all number of different locomotives as the older ex-LMS types were scrapped, including several different examples of the BR Standard classes, notably the Class 4 4-6-0s and 2-6-0s, in the number ranges 75XXX and 76XXX. There were also large numbers

of Stanier 8F 2-8-0s, and a much larger allocation of Class 5 4-6-0s then hitherto. Indeed, in April 1965 Stoke had no less than 76 steam locomotives, at the time second only to Carlisle Kingmoor and Manchester Newton Heath on the LMR. However, this was of but relatively short duration, as the never ending encroachment of diesels, largely BR Sulzer and BR AEI Type 2s (Later Class 24 and 25) from Crewe, took over all the jobs, leading to the closure of Stoke shed on 6 August 1967. The closure was among the last in the country, and only a year before steam's final demise, in August 1968. Ironically, in days gone by, early August provided the busiest weekends of the year, with the traditional 'Wakes' holidays beginning; such was the changing pattern of life!

Today the area is but a shadow of its former self, with little but the main lines remaining. The double track electrified route still exists from Macclesfield via Stoke to both Stone and Colwich, and there are locals operated by Central Trains and main line trains operated by Virgin Cross Country and Virgin West Coast. However, little remains in the way of sidings anywhere, and apart from a small amount of opencast coal, and Silverdale Colliery served by the remaining section of the Market Drayton branch (closed in December 1998) all the district's collieries are no more. Shelton Steel Works remains at Etruria, albeit only a rolling mill now, served by a realigned Grange branch running from Grange Junction north of Etruria. Steel billets arrive by rail from Scunthorpe and many of the rolled sections leave by rail too. The Crewe to Kidsgrove section is still is use, but singled now between Alsager and Crewe North Stafford Sidings and the former connection from there, direct to Basford Hall Marshalling Yards, is no more. From Stoke Junction the two track line still exists to Willington Junction, west of Derby, the greater part of it still signalled by the absolute block system. It is one of the few passenger routes in the country still to retain this method today, and a number of former NSR signal boxes survive for this purpose. Stoke, therefore, still sees quite an extensive passenger service, but there is not much freight apart from the Shelton traffic these days. Services on the Derby route are operated by Central Trains.

As well as this, the track remains in situ from Stoke Junction, via Milton, to Leek Brook, and onwards to Caldon Quarry, but it has seen virtually no traffic since the late 1980s. There is the possibility of renewed stone traffic from the quarry at Caldon, once railway owned and famous for its railway ballast – hence its retention. The section from Leek Brook Junction to Oakamoor has recently been sold to the North Staffordshire Railway (1978) Limited, a preservation movement with its Headquarters at Cheddleton. Part of the track remains on the Cheadle branch, but for what reason I know not.

The Down 'Comet', London to Manchester, and due away from Stoke at 1.2pm, emerging from the main Harecastle Tunnel on Saturday 26 September 1960 in charge of Longsight EE Type 4 D215. Note the splitting distants for Kidsgrove Central Junction, the right-hand one for the Crewe line, and the banner repeater for the Chatterley Junction Down distant. (Michael Mensing)

CHAPTER ONE
THE MAIN LINE

The 'Main Line' of the NSR ran thirty miles and fifty-six chains from Macclesfield to Norton Bridge north of Stafford and at both extremities made connection with the LNWR. The latter's line from Cheadle Hulme, on the Manchester and Birmingham route to Macclesfield, had opened on 24 November 1845 and later made its way onwards (by means of a short tunnel) to a terminus (named Hibel Road with the arrival of the NSR) on 18 June 1849. The southern extremity of the North Stafford was at Norton Bridge, part of the Great Junction Railway (GJR) main line opened between Birmingham and Newton (near Warrington) on 4 July 1837.

The GJR main line skirted the Pottery towns some six miles or so to the west, but a connecting coach service was provided along the Shrewsbury-Newcastle-under-Lyme turnpike road (present A53) with a station established at Whitmore (actually Baldwins Gate, one mile to the west). On its way south the NSR main line passed through Congleton, Kidsgrove, Longport, Etruria, Stoke-on-Trent, Trentham and Stone; it was authorised under one of the original three NSR Acts of 1846, and opened in sections:

Stoke-Norton Bridge	17 April 1848
Stoke-Congleton	9 October 1848
Congleton-Macclesfield	18 June 1849

At Macclesfield, it will be noted, the new line was contiguous with the LNWR; as noted above, that company extended its line to what became a new joint station, known as Macclesfield Hibel Road.

At the same time as the Stoke-Congleton section opened so did the branch from Kidsgrove (known as Harecastle) to Crewe, authorised under the same Act. The Act also authorised a railway of eleven miles and fifty chains from Stone (on the line south to Norton Bridge) running south-east to join the LNWR Trent Valley line at Colwich, six miles twenty-six chains south-east of Stafford. The Trent Valley line of the LNWR, from Rugby to Stafford, had opened 1 December 1847, enabling north to south traffic not needing to call at Birmingham, Wolverhampton or Coventry (or needing to go that way for any other reason) to make a much shorter and quicker journey. It was also of vital strategic importance to the LNWR, in its quest for supremacy in this part of the country. The NSR line to Colwich opened 1 May 1849 and, in effect, became the main line, as most of the through traffic between Manchester and London which went via Stoke traversed this route and missed Stafford. This route not only shortened the distance between Manchester and London, but also the time taken.

The Macclesfield to Stoke section embodied the most significant engineering structures on the entire system, with two impressive viaducts and the Harecastle tunnels. The viaducts, between Congleton and Macclesfield, consisted of a larger one over the River Dane south of North Rode, 1,255ft. long with twenty spans and 106ft. high, and a smaller one 697ft. long with 10 spans and a height of 107ft. This took the line over the Macclesfield Canal, south of its larger sister. Both are of masonry construction and remain in use today.

During the Second World War a large munitions factory, ROF No.5 was established at Swynnerton, between Stone and Norton Bridge. While freight was handled at Badnall Wharf on the ex-LNWR main line north of Norton Bridge, a new railway was built for the many workers' trains. ROF No.5 was the largest of the country's munitions factories during the War, mainly concerned with shell filling, so the passenger traffic was both heavy and designed to accommodate three shift working. Just over a mile long, the branch left the Stone to Norton Bridge line at what became Swynnerton Junction, two miles from Stone. Double track throughout, it terminated at a rather grand four platform station called Cold Meece, opened on 22 July 1941. Though much reduced in numbers, trains continued to run as the factory remained in production after 1945, until closure finally came on 7 June 1958. The signal box at the junction was not abolished, however, until 3 December 1965.

There were three railway tunnels (and five tunnels in all) under Harecastle Hill, where James Brindley had driven his

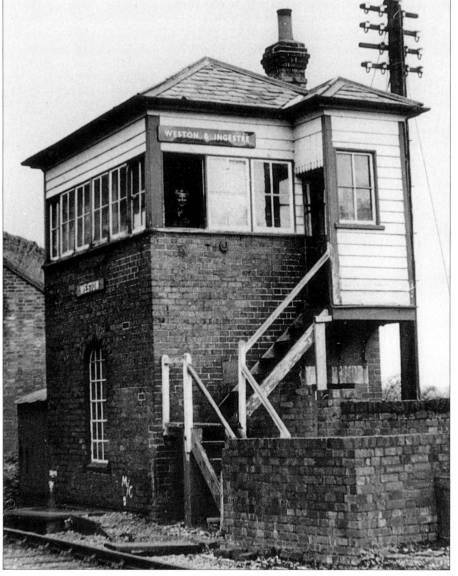

Weston & Ingestre signal box, with the original name of plain Weston on the front; behind is the bridge that replaced an earlier level crossing in 1938. The road is the present A51, Nantwich to Rugeley. Just south of here the Stafford & Uttoxeter Railway crossed the NSR by an overbridge. By the time this photograph was taken in the mid-1950s, the station was long closed, local passenger services having ceased in LMS days, on 6 January 1947. (Author's Collection)

The lines to and from Norton Bridge, looking north towards Stone Junction in 1955. Note the rather splendid station buildings: the tall building to the right with the chimney is the famous Joules Brewery. (Author's Collection)

Grand Trunk Canal (later the Trent & Mersey, completed in 1777). In 1827, Thomas Telford completed a second tunnel, running parallel to the first, on the summit section of the canal. From south to north the railway bores were, successively, the South Tunnel of 1,750 yards, the Middle Tunnel at 180 yards, and the North Tunnel of 130 yards, together with two cuttings, 350 and 333 yards long, between the smaller tunnels. When electrification was being planned, the rela-

tively restricted nature of these tunnels was the principal reason for choosing a new, diversionary route, rather than take the overhead wires through the existing tunnels. The usual course, of increasing the dimensions within the tunnels to accommodate the overhead wires, was complicated by the close proximity of the floor of the south tunnel in relation to the twin canal tunnels which ran almost directly underneath. The engineers considered it dangerous to attempt to deepen the floor

level in the railway tunnels. Every known seam of coal and ironstone in the North Staffordshire coalfield can be found at workable depth in Harecastle Hill, and there had been much uncontrolled working of the seams over very many years. These old workings concealed many hazards and had already presented both railway and canal engineers with severe problems. So a diversionary route, east of the tunnels and through Bathpool, was considered the best option.

Between Stone and Stoke on the Down side of the line was Meaford Power Station, in operation between 1947 and 1991. Actually there were two stations, A and B, and originally served by Barlaston Power Sidings signal box, the junction arrangements latterly being controlled from Stoke power box. This late August 1968 view shows a train of coal arriving behind a brace of BR/Sulzer Type 2s (later Class 24), D5089 leading. The power station locomotive is MEA No.2, a large 18in. cylinder 0-6-0 side tank built by Robert Stephenson & Hawthorns in 1951 (works number 7684) and the Driver Roy Bridgewood. Notice the private owner wagon to left; the wagons allocated to this power station, used to and from local collieries, were among the last private owner coal wagons on the BR system. (Dave Donkin)

The 'Diversion Scheme', almost 2½ miles long, leaves the original route at Chatterley. It necessitated an alteration to the direction of the junction of the Chesterton branch, and rejoins the old route between the North and Middle Tunnels, the former being opened out into a cutting. It includes a short tunnel of 220 yards, a ruling grade for trains leaving Kidsgrove for Stoke of 1 in 80, and 1 in 100 in the opposite direction, so it was no sinecure to operate – especially in the remaining days of steam haulage. Several small lakes (used as reservoirs) in Bathpool Park had to be diverted into one new one on this part of the old Clough Hall estate. This caused much consternation among the locals, in what was considered a local beauty spot. However, a splendid job has been made of landscaping the area, and few complaints are heard these days.

On the opening of the line a generously proportioned roundhouse, with 23 roads,

had fallen out of use some time before this.

In 1864, the NSR entered into an agreement with the Manchester, Sheffield & Lincolnshire Railway (MS&LR – later the Great Central Railway) to build a joint line from Macclesfield, 10 miles and 72 chains to Marple. There it made junction with the MS&LR and Midland Railway joint line from New Mills to Manchester – this was the Macclesfield, Bollington & Marple Railway (MB&MR) and it opened 2 August 1869. At Middlewood, just north of Poynton, a connection was provided with the LNWR line from Buxton to Stockport, which went under the new line and at Macclesfield a new, if temporary, station was built. Originally the two systems were not joined, despite the joint ownership by the NSR, of the MB&MR. It was not until 13 February 1871 that the link was completed and a new station built to serve the joint needs of the NSR and

by virtue of the NSR running powers over the LNWR and provided power mainly for the Churnet Valley line trains. It consisted of a three road straight shed 132ft long, and originally a 40ft. diameter turntable, later replaced by one of 50ft. It closed on 12 June, 1961, with the onslaught of diesel railcars on the local services, but had seen much less use since the through Churnet Valley line passenger services had ended.

All the lines mentioned in this section, with the exception of the MB&MR, the Churnet Valley line and the Swynnerton branch, remain open to both passengers and goods, though there is no local traffic between Stone and Colwich. However, the through Manchester to London trains still use this route, along with some freight.

The NSR arrived at Stafford some time in 1849, under a running powers agreement with the LNWR dated 11 May the previous year. The NSR had opened

The station buildings at Trentham were designed by Sir Charles Barry, Architect to the Duke of Sutherland, to match his nearby Trentham Hall and estate buildings. Although never Directors, the Dukes, 2nd (died 1861) and 3rd, were strong supporters of the NSR and other railways where they had land and property interests. They owned large mineral properties hereabouts, including Florence Colliery in Longton. (FW Shuttleworth)

was built at Stoke, south of the station. This was an extremely imposing building, with a 60 ton overhead travelling crane, capable of traversing the entire building, so that lifting to take place on any road. In this it was unique in British practice. Later, extensive workshops were built alongside but on a lower level, and between the railway and the canal. In the early 1870s a new straight shed, consisting of six roads 260ft. long, was built on the opposite, east side of the line, as the restrictions of the roundhouse became apparent with its 50ft. turntable. However, it was 1929-30 before a 60ft. turntable was provided, the largest Stoke ever had, and this lay nearer the station, by Glebe Street signal box. The former NSR workshops were closed by the LMS in 1926, and the steam shed by BR on 7 August, 1967, although the roundhouse

its new partner. This was Macclesfield Central, six chains north of the junction between the two systems. The existing station used by the NSR and LNWR was renamed Macclesfield Hibel Road at the same time, and thereafter some of the LNWR and NSR through traffic stopped at both Macclesfield stations. The MB&MR was converted to double track, the work being completed on 26 June 1873.

On 7 November 1960 a new station was built at Macclesfield, roughly on the site of Central and replacing both the earlier ones. On that same day Churnet Valley line passenger trains ceased to run and Hibel Road Station was closed. The MB&MR closed, to both passenger and freight traffic, on 5 January 1970.

Macclesfield shed, located north of the station, dates from 1864. It was reached

its first stretch of railway from Stoke, 10¾ miles to Norton Bridge (about 4¾ miles north of Stafford on the original Grand Junction Railway) on 17 May 1848. However, it had to terminate at a temporary station with a dead end bay, as the junction arrangements were not complete. The LNWR station at Norton Bridge was one of the original stations on the route, and it had opened with the line from Stafford to Crewe on 4 July 1837. The NSR Norton Bridge station was alongside the LNWR one it seems, with a footbridge provided for passenger access between the two. Goods traffic was dealt with at Waterbridge, on the NSR line itself, and just on the Stone side of where the two routes converged. Goods traffic in fact appears to have commenced a few days earlier, on 3 May, though everything had to be transhipped between

Trentham, with a Down train entering from the north, hauled by Fowler Class 4 tank No.42318 of Macclesfield shed, on 10 August 1952. Note signal box just visible to the left through the station canopy, and the wagons behind the train in the Florence Colliery Sidings. The dirt tip behind the rear coach is that of Great Fenton Colliery, otherwise known as Stafford, at Sideway. (FW Shuttleworth)

the two systems by hand. The GJR and later the LNWR had been quite indifferent about providing goods facilities here, pointing out to the inhabitants of nearby Eccleshall that, as the station was in a cutting, it would be difficult and expensive. Eventually, they did make suitable arrangements, but some 2½ miles north at Badnall Wharf – this opened in 1843.

Trentham was the junction of the last branch built by the NSR, to Trentham Park; opened 1 April 1910, it was intended to be part of a more ambitious project. Powers were obtained in 1907 for the four mile Trentham, Newcastle-under-Lyme & Silverdale Railway, joining the main line at Trentham with the terminus of the Pool Dam branch off the Market Drayton line. Among other things, it was intended that by this route mineral traffic heading south from the Audley coalfield would avoid Stoke, which had become something of a bottleneck. Despite this, the junction arrangements at Trentham *faced* Stoke, although there was room for a triangular junction if this should later be found necessary. The onset of the First World War put paid to these plans, and as we have seen the branch got no further than Trentham Park, where a station was built. Though the bridge for the extension over the present A34 was constructed, it was never used. This view shows the station at Trentham Junction in 1959, reached by a footpath from the main station. The line lost its regular passenger service in 1927, but was retained for excursion traffic to Trentham Gardens, a local leisure resort after the Duke of Sutherland moved out of the Hall. The last such excursion was on 25 August 1957, official closure coming on 1 October the same year. However, the track was left in situ and was used occasionally for wagon storage, in particular coal wagons in the summer, and was not lifted until the early 1960s. This photograph looks down the branch towards Trentham Park. (Author's Collection)

Trentham Junction in February 1964, looking towards Stoke – Ivatt Class 2 2-6-0 No.46503 of Northwich shed heads south with a short mixed freight. Note on the left the signal box and junction arrangements, and on the right part of the newly developed Hem Heath Colliery. (Dave Donkin)

By 1 December 1849 at least, a proper junction arrangement had been brought into use and trains were running through between the NSR and LNWR. Later, the bay platform line was extended to join the LNWR Up line, making the Up platform an island. Later still, when the line from Stafford to Crewe was quadrupled in March 1876, both platforms became islands, with another added to serve the easternmost Down line. The celebrated penchant for through running soon manifested itself and the August 1868 NSR *Drivers Diagrams* for instance, show NSR engines and men running through to Albion, Bloomfield and Birmingham with goods and mineral traffic. There would appear to have been an NSR locomotive shed at Norton Bridge in early times; certainly the Director's minutes of 1849 make reference to one, with later suggestions in 1861 that it be transferred to Stone. Whether it was or not, has gone unrecorded. The Stafford & Uttoxeter

Hughes/Fowler 'Crab' 42894 of Stoke shed (Stoke had a number of this type allocated in the early 1960s) with coal empties for the Market Drayton line, approaching Newcastle Junction (almost certainly destined for Holditch Colliery) on 15 March 1962. It was always the practice to use tender engines on the Apedale branch that served Holditch Colliery, and for engines to work tender first up the branch, as would be the case here. This and the following photograph are full of interest. From left to right notice: Class 4 tank lifting a train of empty stock from Cockshute Carriage Sidings, Junction signal box, diesel shunter working in Cockshute Sidings, Etruria Gas works, Cockshute Sidings signal box, locomotive water tanks and the original Twyford Sanitary Manufactory. (FW Shuttleworth)

Stoke Class 4 tank No.42378 with empty stock for Cockshute Carriage Sidings, approaching Newcastle Junction from the south on 15 March 1962. The Market Drayton branch curves away at a 1 in 102 gradient to the extreme left, while the goods brake van and wagons are the tail of the train seen in the previous illustration. (FW Shuttleworth)

Railway arrived at Stafford on 23 December 1867, when it opened its line from Bromshall Junction, north of Uttoxeter as noted in the *Derby and Burton Lines* section of this book. This later passed to the Great Northern and was nothing to do with the NSR *per se*.

Other lines at Stafford were the direct Trent Valley line from Rugby, obviating the need for all traffic to go via Birmingham and Wolverhampton, opened on 26 July 1847, and the 29¼ mile Shropshire Railways & Canal Company route from Wellington to Stafford via Newport, opened on 1 June 1849. Leased to the LNWR from July 1847 (before it even opened, be it noted) it was never acquired by the bigger company, remaining 'independent' until the Grouping. By this route the LNWR obtained access to Shrewsbury from the south; with the GWR it jointly owned the line onwards from Wellington to Shrewsbury, and this too, opened 1 June 1849.

Thus Stafford became an important junction, and in LMS and BR days many Birmingham to Manchester trains ran direct, via the NSR. Some of the London to Manchester (via Stoke) expresses that stopped at Stafford, moreover, took the route via Norton Bridge, instead of the direct line from Colwich – and indeed, they still do.

Long time Stoke resident, 4F No.44309, crossing from Down Slow to Down Fast, possibly to take the Loop Line from Etruria Junction, with a down mixed freight in 1963. The train is alongside the island platform at Etruria (this was one of very few island platforms on the NSR, and the third station at Etruria – the earlier two had a conventional arrangement). Twyford's new sanitary ware factory can be seen to the right, with Etruria Gas Works to the left. The buildings behind the train are the former workshops of WR Renshaw & Co., Ltd., engineers and railway wagon builders. The famous Barnam & Bailey travelling circus train consisting of vans, flat wagons and coaches, was built at this works around the turn of the century, and this was also its winter quarters – the siding connection was always known to local railwaymen as 'Barnams Siding' well into living memory. (MG Fell)

View looking south from Chatterley towards Bradwell Sidings with Austerity 8F 2-8-0 90457 of Mirfield Shed (way off its normal haunts) heading north with a mixed freight on 12 April 1962. Bradwell Sidings signal box in the right distance is still in use today and, as can be seen, there were four tracks here. There were Up and Down Slow lines continuously between Chatterley and Longport Junction, and from Grange Junction to Stoke Junction. Part of the Staffordshire Chemical Company's works can be seen behind the train. This Company had operations on both sides of the main line, and its locomotives had running powers to cross the main lines with internal traffic. The signal in the foreground, an NSR McKenzie & Holland original, was to control these moves, opposite to the normal traffic on this, the Down slow line. (FW Shuttleworth)

The Stafford & Uttoxeter line closed as a through route on 5 March 1951, though the stub at Stafford survived to serve the RAF 16 Maintenance Unit (closed 1 December 1975) and a number of other private sidings. The line to Wellington closed to passengers on 7 September 1964, and freight 1 July 1968. However, on 31 December 1962 the wholly rebuilt station had been officially opened at Stafford, as a part of the London Midland Region modernisation and electrification of the main lines from London to Manchester and Liverpool. Norton Bridge station remains open, the only intermediate station between Stafford and Crewe, though it is now served only by Stafford to Stoke local services. Under the route modernisation plans, the main line platforms were removed – it's a four track section here – and new signalling arrangements came into use in October 1961. There was also a new island platform to serve the Stoke line, and the main line junction with the slow lines was removed. Crossover roads were provided south of the station, together with a by-

Chatterley again, this time looking in the opposite direction, north towards Harecastle Tunnel with a Up train of empty coal wagons approaching behind 4F No.44299 of Stoke Shed, on 12 April 1962. Just discernible to the extreme left is the home signal protecting the Talke and Chesterton branches, and at the rear of the train can be seen Chatterley Junction signal box. To the right of this is Goldendale Ironworks, and to the right of the engine the site of Ravensdale Ironworks. The building is the former Port Vale public house, and the football club of that name originally played nearby, hence the Club's name. The word Port came from the location near to the Trent & Mersey Canal, which runs in a shallow cutting in the right background. (FW Shuttleworth)

The Harecastle Diversion scheme under way and just before completion, looking north at Chatterley. This view clearly illustrates the route the new line takes west of Harecastle Hill, and around the high ground through Bathpool. Note realigned route of the Chesterton branch left foreground, and its former route bisected by the new line – between the two can be seen the remains of the blowing engine house of the old Chatterley Ironworks, closed in 1901. Also to be seen, going under the main lines just where the new line leaves the old, is the partly filled-in remains of the Chatterley Branch Canal and Basin, built to serve the needs of the ironworks. To the right of the line is the old Port Vale pub. In the apex between old and new lines is the then quite new NCB Chatterley Coal Stocking Ground, intended to hold coal stocks from local collieries in the summer months. A small coal stock can be seen along with the railway sidings. This site was intended to be much larger, and a shed was built to house the NCB locomotives – this can be seen just to the right of the new line. In the event it was never used and shunting was undertaken by the main line engines. The site soon fell out of use as the output of the local collieries reduced. Chatterley Junction signal box can be seen alongside the original line, with the Goldendale Ironworks sidings curving away to the right. The period is about April 1966. (Collection MG Fell)

Stoke Class 4 2-6-4T No.42603 with an up train of coal empties, passing Chatterley on 12 April 1962. Goldendale Ironworks slag tips to right, with slag reduction plant just above the engine. (FW Shuttleworth)

Looking north, the Harecastle Tunnel Diversion line veers off to the left with the old main lines still in situ beyond – 29 August 1967. Chatterley Junction signal box, still in use as a shunting frame, can just be seen in the right distance. To the left is the realigned Chesterton branch, with 08 shunter D4109 bringing a train of coal wagons from Parkhouse Colliery towards Bradwell Sidings. The building remains behind are those of the old Chatterley ironworks, and the building in the centre, just beyond the new line, is the engine shed – never used – of the NCB Chatterley Coal Stocking Ground.
(MG Fell)

directional recess line, so that stopping trains to and from Stoke did not have to occupy the main line when calling at the station. The old NSR signal box at Waterbridge, which had by then been renamed 'North Stafford Sidings', had ceased to be a block post on 16 August 1931, and was replaced entirely under the new arrangements. The goods station itself had closed on 22 June 1959.

There was an LNWR engine shed at Stafford, dating from about 1852. This closed officially on 19 July 1965, but was retained as a signing on point for loco-motive men for some time after this, and indeed locomotives and multiple units continued to be stabled there. The No.2 shed – until the 1930s there had been two shed buildings – was reroofed in 1947 and survives to this day as industrial

premises. The Great Northern-owned Stafford & Uttoxeter Railway had its own shed at Stafford Common, but it would appear that after the Grouping in 1923, arrangements were made for engines to be stabled and serviced at the former LNWR shed. Likewise, whatever facili-ties the NSR engines needed at Stafford, always seem to have been provided by the LNWR.

A view south along the Chatterley Valley from the site, almost, of Chatterley Station (closed 27 September 1948) on 23 April 1966, showing the 5.57pm Derby to Crewe DMU. This is a three car Craven unit, with the local B6 headcode for such workings. To the extreme left can be seen the Goldendale Ironworks, and between it and the railway the Trent & Mersey Canal. The tall chimney to right of centre marks the site of Peake's Tilery Colliery, east of the main line, and the twin towers on the skyline are the winding houses of the redeveloped Wolstanton Colliery, south of Longport. (Michael Mensing)

Up freight heading south at Chatterley on 28 September 1963, having just left Harecastle Tunnel. 44048, despite a Derby shedplate, was allocated to Uttoxeter at this time – this shed generally had a 4F on its allocation, ostensibly for working freight along the Churnet Valley line, but the engine is well off its normal haunts here. They were extremely common in the area, and Stoke had a substantial complement from quite early LMS days. The signal is the Chatterley Junction, Down advanced starter. (Michael Mensing)

Down empty coaching stock and parcels train leaving the Middle Harecastle Tunnel, heading north on 26 September 1960. The engine is Aston Class 4 tank No.42470. The private Birchenwood Colliery line to reach its Bathpool estate ran on the top of the cutting to the left, roughly in line with the telegraph poles. (Michael Mensing)

Short up freight between the North and Middle Harecastle Tunnels on 26 September 1960, hauled by Stoke 4F No.44536 – the signal is the Kidsgrove Central Junction Up advanced starter. The later Harecastle Tunnel diversion line left the formation of this line on the left, roughly opposite the engine. (Michael Mensing)

A view in the summer of 1966, looking down from above the Diversion line, and towards where the previous photograph was taken. A southbound three car Craven DMU is just about to enter the Middle Harecastle Tunnel, with a Crewe to Derby working. The new line, rising at 1 in 80, can be seen in the foreground together with the new, 200 yard tunnel. The Diversion line was two and a half miles long. (Dave Donkin)

The Harecastle Diversion Line, looking north on 26 April 1975. The train is the 14.20 Crewe to Derby and Lincoln, consisting of a three car Swindon built 'Cross Country' DMU (later Class 120). A number were allocated to Derby Etches Park at this time, and were used on these services. Note to the right the signs of earlier mineral workings and the public roadway built through the Bathpool Park, as some compensation for the railway passing this way. The train is approaching the bridge, which takes the Peacocks Hay to Talke road over the railway. Harecastle Hill is to the right. (Michael Mensing)

Congleton Upper Junction on 30 May 1954, looking south. The connecting spur with the Biddulph Valley line is on the left, still protected by McKenzie & Holland NSR signals. On this occasion the junction signal box was switched out, and all main line signals are clear – the one in the middle is the junction Up starter, with the Congleton Up distant underneath. Note the sharp gradient of the connecting spur, 1 in 45. This connecting line was last used on 25 November 1963 (and 'officially' taken out of use on 1 December 1963) for sand traffic which normally travelled via the Biddulph Valley line to Stoke. However, on this occasion flooding of the line at Ford Green prevented through traffic. (Late Dr JR Hollick)

Western side of Congleton viaduct, 8 April 1962. This was the southernmost of the two viaducts on the line between Kidsgrove and Macclesfield, taking the line over Bath Vale, through which passed the Macclesfield Canal (Congleton to the left and Macclesfield to the right). The scaffolding under two of the arches was for repair work. In the foreground is the Biddulph Valley line climbing up from Brunswick Wharf, itself to the right. (FW Shuttleworth)

North Rode Junction on 31 May 1957, looking north towards the station and Macclesfield. Main line to the left, Churnet valley line to the right – the signal box was in the apex behind the photographer. (Late Dr JR Hollick)

The south end of the station, in the mid-1950s. The working of some of the Manchester to London trains via Stoke goes back to an LNWR and NSR agreement of 1866, following years of 'fighting'. The mighty LNWR had harboured aspirations for many years to acquire what was, in its view, an impudent upstart of a railway. It thought to swallow up the NSR like many another such company. However, the LNW bargained without the fighting spirit of the local North Staffordshire folk, who having failed to get the LNWR or its predecessors to build a railway through the area, were not going to give their own away, at least without a struggle. Amazingly, they won their battle and after the 1866 agreement the two companies worked together so harmoniously that their relations became the envy of a number of other companies who had to live with the might of Euston! The NSR and LNW shared extensive running powers over each other's systems and a share of the London to Manchester traffic was routed via Macclesfield and Stoke, with the NSR working the trains from Manchester to Stoke.

Looking north in the mid-1950s. The line to the left went to the goods yard, which lay on the west side of the station. The local Fowler 2-6-4T No.42320 is performing some sort of shunting operation.

CHAPTER TWO
STOKE

Stoke-upon-Trent itself was of course, the hub of the NSR, and where its headquarters were located. It was also the site of its principal locomotive shed and carriage and wagon workshops. Of all the smaller British railway companies, the NSR was unique in the extent to which it built its own locomotives and rolling stock, and in later years it was largely self sufficient. Indeed, apart from the narrow gauge engines, three rail motors and a pair of locos bought at a knock-down rate as a result of a cancelled order, it built all its own locomotives at Stoke from 1905 until the end of its existence. Indeed, apart from just sixteen out of a total of 118, it built all its own requirements in the thirty years before that.

In 1910, by means of 'Federation', the six towns and sixty villages of this enclave of North Staffordshire came together as the Borough of Stoke-on-Trent. The six towns combined to form one administration, though some local powers were retained along with a number of elected representatives, rather along the lines of parish councils. It was the Act of Parliament of 1908, coming into force on 31 March 1910, which created the County Borough of Stoke-on-Trent. Stoke itself

is Stoke-*upon*-Trent. The six towns, from south to north, were Longton, Fenton, Stoke-upon-Trent, Hanley, Burslem and Tunstall, in a locality world-famous then as now, for its pottery and similar wares. Nowhere else in the United Kingdom is anywhere known so universally by it products, for most people know what part of the country is concerned when the Potteries are talked about. In 1926 the late King George V (during a visit) conferred on the 'Federation' the status of City – at the time the only one in the British Isles without a cathedral. In its early days the 'Federation' was a difficult one, and it took the good Burghers of the six towns a long time to come to grips with their loss of independence – even today, the six very proud-looking Town Halls stand as a reminder of earlier times.

The construction of Stoke Station, a grand affair, together with the rather magnificent roundhouse for the engines, was delayed until after the first services started to operate, those to Norton Bridge commencing on 17 April 1848. A temporary station had to serve, at Whieldon Grove, south of the eventual site and adjacent to the roundhouse. The main station came into use on 9 October 1848, at

the same time as the line north to Congleton opened. The roundhouse was not fully complete until 1852, but doubtless parts were available earlier. The temporary station, which occupied a much older and rather dignified old house, Whieldon Grove, became the offices of the Locomotive Department, and a grand one at that. It survived as the local Motive Power Department Offices, doubtless the most grandiose in the country, until the shed closed in 1967.

Stoke Station was rather unusual in that it had only two through platforms, along with two centre roads that (at least in pre-grouping days) were largely used for stabling of coaching stock – they served for through traffic later. True, after a time there appeared a two platform bay at the north end and on the Down side (later reduced to one platform) but this only served the Market Drayton line trains. Most, if not all, the other services were through trains, and even the bulk of the Loop Line trains continued to destinations south of Stoke. By means of permissive block working two and on occasions, three, trains could be accommodated simultaneously on each of the long platform faces. It was always quite an

'Fifties spotters add up their haul outside the station, oblivious of the cars and taxis. The station square remains a curiously quiet and dignified place to this day.

Stoke station looking south in the early 1950s. Note Glebe Street Signal Box visible through the station, and between the two tank engines Newcastle bay to the right.

Stoke station frontage, former NSR Directors' Board Room immediately above the central doorway, again in the early 1950s.

Manchester to London express entering Stoke from the north during the first week of electric working of these trains, in March 1967. The locomotive is one of the Class AL3s (later Class 83) built by English Electric, and shortly to be put in to store in view of persistent rectifier problems. This was possible as delivery of the new Class 86 locomotives was getting under way at the time. Later, in 1972-73, they were refurbished with solid state rectification, and returned to service as the line from Crewe to Glasgow was being electrified. (Dave Donkin)

Class 5 4-6-0 No.44853 of Leeds Holbeck, and doubtless on an ex-works running in turn, leaving Stoke for the north with a local passenger train on 10 August 1952. This would probably be a Derby to Crewe working; some were Crewe North diagrams, and they were often used for engines recently off Crewe Works, as 'running in' turns. (FW Shuttleworth)

Another view of the north end of Stoke station, on 10 August 1960. The bay platform to the right, roofed over in 1892, was originally for trains using the Newcastle and Market Drayton line, earning thus it sobriquet, the 'Newcastle Bay'. Notice the young 'spotters' on the goods dock in front of the engine to left, DMU in Up platform, and Glebe Street signal box seen through the overall roof. Other than the bay, Stoke relied on its two long platforms and by using permissive block working, two and on occasions three trains could be accommodated on each platform simultaneously. In normal circumstances, it was only for the London-Manchester through trains that the entire platform faces were necessary. As the famous novelist, and chronicler of 'Five Towns' life so aptly put in what is perhaps his finest novel, *The Old Wives' Tale*: 'The express from London was late, so that Constance had three-quarters of an hour of the stony calmness of Knype (Stoke) platform when it is waiting for a great train'.

event, and to some extent still is, when the through London to Manchester expresses arrived, and a complete platform had to be kept clear. *'The express from London was late, so that Constance had three quarters of an hour of the stony calmness of Knype [Stoke] platform when it is waiting for a great train'*, wrote the Nineteenth Century novelist, Arnold

Bennett in his classic, *The Old Wives' Tale*.

The workshops, at a lower level than the main line, lay west of the railway and alongside the Trent & Mersey Canal, reached by a steeply graded line which left the Biddulph Valley line at Pratts Sidings. They date from not long after the formation of the company, and were

added to over the years. Despite their cramped surroundings, some magnificent work was undertaken, and locomotives were built there from 1868. Despite closure by the LMS in 1926, most of the buildings survive today, as industrial premises.

The roundhouse was augmented by an LNWR-style straight shed opened in the

View looking north from approximately the centre of Stoke station on 10 August 1960, over the enormously extended water 'column' provided for up trains. The plates between the rails indicate the course of the subways. The entrance arch for passengers was the NSR War Memorial, in memory of the 1,423 men of the railway who served with the armed forces (about a quarter of the total staff) and the 146 who made the supreme sacrifice – their names all being displayed in raised letters on cast bronze plaques. The arch is made of local Hollington (near Cheadle) stone, and was unveiled by the Chairman of the Company, Lord Anslow (Tonman Mosley 1850-1933, Chairman 1904-1923) on 15 August 1922, and stands to this day.

Stoke station interior looking south, the opposite way from the previous illustration, but from the same spot, also on 10 August 1960. Glebe Street signal box to left, goods shed to right. There was no subway at this end of the station, and the bridge shown was for goods only, served by the exposed lift shafts. Notice the young train spotters on the Down platform, a place to frequently find the Author, at about this time.

Glebe Street signal box on 10 August 1960, looking east – at one time this box was known as Stoke South – Glebe Street passes under the railway by the bridge girder seen to extreme right. In earlier times there had been a level crossing here, and the low bridge that replaced it must have been the most frequently hit by road vehicles in the locality. It still happens today, despite the warning given to road users. This box contained a 67 lever McKenzie & Holland frame when built, but was replaced by one of standard BR pattern during the 1950s.

South end of the straight shed at Stoke with the remains of its original roof on 6 September 1953. This six road shed was built in the LNWR Ramsbottom style and dates from the early 1870s. The right-hand section lost its roof early in the 1930s, but the BR pattern one seen here was not erected until the early 1950s, the work having been suspended during the War. The two road lean-to type building to the left was built to house the rail motors and dates from 1905. Long-time Stoke residents visible include, from left to right, Class 4 tanks Nos.42670 and 42668 and Class 4F No.44383. Note roundhouse to left, separated by the Biddulph, Derby, and main lines. (FW Shuttleworth)

1870s, on the opposite side of the main line. This had six roads in two separate, but adjacent buildings, and was sixty yards long. Over the years it was added to, with a full length single road lean-to type extension appearing on the east side in about 1890. When the rail motors arrived in 1905, a much shorter two road shed, forty yards long, was added on the western wall. In 1929-30, a new 60ft.

turntable was installed, but due to space restrictions, this was near the station at Glebe Street and was reached by the Viaduct Sidings, which ran parallel to the main lines between shed and station. Hitherto, the only means of turning engines was the 50ft. table in the roundhouse, and with the larger engines arriving on the scene, this made for some severe restrictions. There had been an

another 50ft. table, on the west side of the station, reached by the goods yard. It dated from 1865, but fell out of use following goods yard extensions around the turn of the century. In 1936, a 150 ton capacity mechanical coaling plant was erected to serve the shed, together with mechanical ash disposal equipment.

With the introduction of diesel multiple units on local passenger services, a

The remains of the roundhouse on 6 September 1953, bereft of its original roof. The 50ft diameter turntable greatly restricted the sizes of locomotive that could use this building, but as the North Stafford was very much a tank engine railway, this was not too much of a problem in its day. The biggest tender engines that could be accommodated were the Ivatt and Standard Class 4 2-6-0s which Stoke had a few of in later years. Here is 4F No.44310, a Stoke engine for many years, with 2-6-4T No.42671 just about to leave. The NSR ground disc – unusual to see signals *inside* engine sheds – was interlocked with the turntable, and protected movements when not set for the relevant road. (FW Shuttleworth)

The south end of the straight shed, with the former 'motor' shed to the left, by this time (with its roof surviving) housing the breakdown train. Apart from the Class 3F tank – about the only one surviving here by this date – the engines are typical of Stoke's latter day allocation, Ivatt Class 4 2-6-0s and a Standard Class 2 2-6-0, No.78017. The BR Standard 350 hp 0-6-0 diesel shunters had been around the area since the late 1950s, and performed most shunting jobs by this date, 23 April 1966. (Dave Donkin)

new maintenance depot was built for them at Cockshute Sidings, north of the station. This was the site of the principal carriage maintenance facilities, by the junction with the Market Drayton line. A three road depot 454ft. long was built, with capacity for six three car units; it came into use in October 1957. As well as railcars, it also catered for the small

fleet of diesel shunting locomotives (350HP 0-6-0 later Class 08 and 09) that had started to replace steam on a few of the local shunting and trip duties, but by and large, local workings remained with steam haulage until almost the end of steam working in this country. Indeed, Stoke steam shed outlasted Cockshute, which became superfluous with the on-

set of electrification, and closed on 6 April 1966. The building however, survives, in industrial use.

Stoke shed itself lingered on, and did not close completely until 7 August 1967. Despite suggestions that the roundhouse should be preserved, even in view of its by then rather dilapidated condition, this was not to be. It was demolished in 1970,

The steel lattice overhead traversing ash handling plant, built in 1936, was of unusual design and could serve three roads. Others of similar construction generally served less roads, or were of reinforced concrete. On 18 February 1967 9F No.92084 of Birkenhead stands alongside Stoke's own Class 5, No.45003. The 2-10-0s were frequent visitors to Stoke at this time, always from Birkenhead's allocation, with imported iron ore trains for Shelton steelworks. (Dave Donkin)

Another 1967 view of the mechanical coaler, with the legs of the ash handling plant in the foreground. The building on the extreme left housed the Motive Power Offices, formerly the temporary Stoke station, when the NSR first opened. This was Whieldon Grove, an 18th Century two storey mansion sometimes known as Fenton Hall. A rather splendid building in its day, it had been the home of one Thomas Whieldon 1719-1795. It was semi-derelict by 1849, and thus formed an ideal temporary station until the permanent one was completed in October 1848. Unfortunately, together with the roundhouse it was demolished about 1970. (Dave Donkin)

together with all the other buildings, including the former Whieldon Grove House, which was a great pity, and the site was cleared. In 1961, a new freight terminal was opened at Stoke, to concentrate goods transhipment and delivery arrangements in the area. This replaced the old goods sheds at Hanley, Longport, Longton, Newcastle, Leek, Stone, Congleton and Stafford, although arrangements for wagon loads remained available at some of them. The bonded store at Hanley, which also closed, was

replaced by facilities in the old Stoke goods shed, adjacent to the station. The new concentration terminal, on the Down side north of the station and alongside Newcastle Junction, where the Market Drayton line left the main line, covered 17½ acres. The shed itself, 460ft. by 404ft., covered six acres and a fleet of road vehicles made the collections and deliveries, with the initial daily traffic consisting of 150 loaded railway wagons in, and 200 out. They were worked by one of the new diesel shunting locomotives.

Beer traffic from Burton-on-Trent was also dealt with here. Alas, with the general run down of freight traffic on the railway, both this establishment and Stoke goods yard itself closed in the 1980s. The railways of course gradually came out of the collection and delivery and wagon load business, and today there are almost no sidings of any description at Stoke. The station consists of the two long platforms, as it always has, with one remaining bay at the north end, and an Up through road.

A few days before the end of steam at Stoke, this picture was taken on 2 August 1967. Most of the engines are dead, their fires having been drawn for the last time, but on the left Class 8F No.48375, behind it an Ivatt Class 4, and the Standard Class 4 No.75018 to the right, are in steam. The picture was taken about mid-day. I was working in the Stoke Divisional Offices at the time and wandered down to the shed at lunchtime, during this last week of steam working to have an almost final look. Class 8F 48131 is out of steam on the right. View looks north. The last 'official' day of steam at Stoke was Sunday 6 August 1967, and found but a handful of engines in steam, most of which would do no more than run light to Crewe the following day. However, Birkenhead 9F No.92109, which had brought a load of iron ore from Bidston Dock to Shelton Steelworks on the previous Saturday morning, would return with the empties the following day. This was not only the last such working steam hauled, but also the last booked steam turn off Stoke shed. But, in the best plans of mice and men, flooding of the Biddulph Valley line between Milton Junction and Ford Green, meant that the Type 2 diesels drafted in to replace steam, could not operate over this section, to serve Norton, Chatterley Whitfield and Victoria Collieries. So a few engines were retained and continued to work this section for about two months. After Stoke closed to steam, if any 9Fs appeared on the iron ore workings (which they continued to do for a few weeks) they had to come off at Crewe, and be replaced by a diesel. (Allan C Baker)

The magnificent Jacobean style frontage of Stoke station, the work of an otherwise unknown architect, R.A. Stent. The station stands in what became known as Winton Square (after the famous potter) and was complemented opposite by the North Stafford Hotel, flanked by its twin matching houses. All dated from the opening of the railway, and all exist to this day as some of the finest examples of railway architecture of the period. This picture and other similar views date from the middle 1950s, the whole façade having since been very much cleaned up. The large window in the centre of the station marks the NSR Board Room.

The North Stafford Hotel, directly opposite the station entrance in Winton Square, 21 October 1933. This view shows to good effect the architecture of R.A. Stent, assisted by the famous H.A. Hunt. The hotel opened in 1849 and after considerable extension in 1878 had 130 bedrooms. Passing to the LMS at Grouping it was sold out of railway ownership in January 1953 and remains to this day, as befits its parentage, the finest hotel in the locality. (Authors Collection)

Rolleston signal box on the line between Marston Junction and Burton North Stafford Junction. By the time this photograph was taken on 20 September 1952 the box was closed. This line closed to passenger traffic with the last 'Tutbury Jenny' in June 1960 and completely on 30 October 1966. (FW Shuttleworth)

Millfield Junction, looking south with the Longton, Adderley Green & Bucknall Railway curving away to the left, by this time truncated and only serving Park Hall Colliery. From later NSR days this was always known as Normacot Junction, and the down Normacot station platform can be seen from this up train. The branch by this time was known as the Park Hall Colliery branch. It ceased to be used on closure of Park Hall Colliery, on 23 December 1962, although it was not officially taken out of use until July 1964, as a little traffic continued to flow to a landsale wharf at Meir Hay which was served by the branch. The signal box was abolished in August 1965, the station at Normacot having closed on 2 March 1964. Originally the junction was further north, at Millfield Crossing, with the branch line running alongside the main line until the point of divergence. This arrangement was altered on 25 September 1882, with the opening of a direct connection between main line and branch, and a new signal box known as Normacot Junction was opened. Millfield Junction then became Millfield Crossing, as it controlled a level crossing. This signal box and sidings were established in July 1870, to serve the private siding of W H Sparrow, who owned Millfield Lane Colliery, east of the line. Later the box ceased to be a block post, and disappeared altogether when the level crossing was replaced by a bridge – despite this, many still referred to the junction as Millfield Junction. (Collection Paul Knapper)

CHAPTER THREE
DERBY and BURTON LINES

The original NSR Acts also granted powers to build a line from Stoke to Burton-on-Trent, via the southern Pottery towns of Fenton and Longton and thence to Meir, Cresswell, Uttoxeter, Sudbury and Tutbury to join the Midland route from Derby to Birmingham. Laying just 58 chains east of Burton-on-Trent station, this became Burton Junction, on a line which had opened on 12 August 1839, the NSR having running powers over the Midland Railway into Burton-on-Trent. The NSR line opened to Uttoxeter on 7 August 1848 and onwards to Burton 11 September the same year. Later, on 1 April 1868, a branch was built from Stretton Junction (62 chains before Burton NS Junction) just over a mile to Hawkins Lane Junction, gaining access (by running powers) to the LNWR goods depot at Horninglow and thus a share of the premium Burton beer traffic. The NSR also had running powers over the LNWR and MR, to gain access to Bond Road goods depot, for similar purposes.

In 1849, the NSR acquired powers to build a line, four miles 38 chains long, from Marston Junction (on the Burton line, one mile 42 chains south of Tutbury) to join the same MR Derby-Burton line, but this time facing Derby, at what became Willington Junction. This was five miles and 29 chains from Derby station, the NSR also having running powers into Derby. Engine sheds were established at Burton and Derby in 1865 and the late

1870s respectively; up to then NSR engines had been housed in the Midland Railway sheds. However, for reasons of economy, within months of the Grouping the NSR sheds closed – Burton on 6 July 1923, and Derby on 30 June 1923 – and thereafter the Knotty engines could be found at either the former Midland Shed at Derby, or the former Midland and LNWR sheds at Burton.

The NSR line to Willington Junction passed through Eggington. Much later, on 1 April 1878 (though goods traffic appears to have commenced as early as 24 January) the Great Northern Railway opened a line from Derby, via Mickleover to Eggington, where it made junction with the NSR facing Stoke. This came about through joint aspirations with the Stafford & Uttoxeter Railway, an independent concern, which had completed its twelve miles from Stafford to Bromshall Junction, a couple of miles west of Uttoxeter, on 23 December, 1867. Connection was made with the LNWR at Stafford. Running powers were granted over the NSR, between Eggington Junction and Bromshall Junction, and through working from Nottingham to Stafford commenced. The GNR took over the ailing Stafford & Uttoxeter in August 1881. A spur was opened by the GNR between Eggington Junction and Dove Junction on the NSR Burton line, on 1 May 1878. This allowed through running by GNR trains between

Derby and Burton, the GNR having running powers over the NSR thence to Burton.

Another branch left the NSR Derby and Burton lines, to Cheadle, south east of the Potteries and east of the main line. It had a very chequered history, opening in stages to reach Cheadle on 1 January 1901 – three miles 71 chains long, it left the main line at Cresswell. Originally an 'independent' concern, known as the Cheadle Railway, it was absorbed by the NSR on 1 January 1907, though it was always operated by the North Stafford. There was also the Longton, Adderley Green & Bucknall Railway; another nominally independent concern, it opened its three miles and 54 chains of route, forming a loop between the Biddulph Valley line at Botteslow Junction and the Burton and Derby line at Normacot, in September 1875. A goods and mineral only railway, it served a number of collieries. Lastly, at Uttoxeter, a junction was made with yet another line authorised by the original NSR Acts, the Churnet Valley route connecting North Rode on the main line south of Macclesfield with Uttoxeter, via Leek. This line was 27 miles and 54 chains of double track and opened 13 July, 1849.

The Burton & Derby line left Stoke by steep gradients, as it climbed to Caverswall, ruling at 1 in 100 for exactly four miles. Banking assistance was usually provided for goods and mineral

Standard Class 4 4-6-0 No.75062 of Stoke shed, heading south and climbing the almost continuous 1 in 100 from Stoke Junction to Caverswall, just south of Normacot on 7 November 1964. The signal above the train is the Normacot Junction up home, for despite the Park Hall branch having closed by this time, the box was still open. Stoke accumulated quite a collection of BR Standard engines in its latter days, including a surprisingly large number of this particular type. (Dave Donkin)

Top right. Meir Station, just south of the 847 yard tunnel, and a few yards short of the summit of the 1 in 100 climb from Stoke. This was the longest tunnel on the NSR apart from Harecastle. The train is the 5.37pm Crewe Works to Cresswell, actually running as empty stock from Stoke, departing 6.25pm, despite the 'lazy' crew not having changed the head lamp code. This train dates from the 1926 closure of Stoke Works, and the transfer of many of the men to Crewe, when a special train was provided running to and from a special platform within the old Carriage Works – latterly the site of the Electric Traction Depot. The stock for this working was kept at Cresswell, where the Cheadle branch left the main line, and despite running as an advertised train in the morning from there to Crewe Station it then continued into the Works, unadvertised for obvious reasons. In the evening it ran unadvertised, and an hour earlier on Fridays to suit the Works hours. It is seen here in September 1965, with Crewe Class 5 No.44681, which would return light from Cresswell to Stoke shed later. This train provided a local steam passenger working ten years after the introduction of DMUs on just about everything else, and remained so worked until late 1966. Later, after a period with EE Type 4 diesels, it became a DMU working, still going to and from the Works, and finally ceased running in 1978. (Dave Donkin)

Right. Blythe Bridge station looking north on 30 October 1966, with the level crossing taking the A50 Stoke-on-Trent to Derby road across the railway. Note the distinctive and high McKenzie & Holland signal box – the other smaller box to be discerned in the distance is Foxfield Colliery Sidings, not a block post, but a shunting frame released from Blythe Bridge box. This colliery was served by a three and a ½ mile long private mineral line dating from 1893. The colliery closed in August 1965, but the line still exists in the ownership of The Foxfield Light Railway Society Limited, a preservation society, and parts of it see use by passenger trains operated by the Society. (Allan C Baker)

Stallington, looking south on 30 October 1966, with the level crossing keepers house, which predates the signal box and block post, on the left. The box was brought in to use on 28 October 1884, and the section to Blythe Bridge became one of the shortest block sections on the NSR system. (Allan C Baker)

Cresswell was the junction with the three mile 71 chain single track branch to Cheadle, west of the main line and opened in stages between 1892 and 1901. Losing its passenger services together with several other local lines on 17 June 1963, the branch remained open largely for sand traffic until 1988. This view on 9 April 1981 shows the empty sand wagons departing from the junction sidings for Cheadle behind an AEI/Sulzer Class 25 diesel. By this date the main line junction has been removed and access to the branch is via the sidings. The station here closed 7 November 1966, along with many others on the line, and was demolished some years later. (Paul Knapper)

Three car BRCW (later Class 104) DMU on the 12-35pm Saturdays only Stoke to Cheadle, on 19 August 1961. Photographed just north of Tean on the diversion line, the old route can just be made out in a cutting following the row of trees to the upper left, and the left of the clump of trees in the centre. (Michael Mensing)

trains. This section includes the 847 yard Meir tunnel. The line to Derby remains in use, and retains its passenger service, but all the branches have long since closed. First to go was the Stafford & Uttoxeter, closing completely beyond Stafford Common on 5 March 1951, though it had lost its passenger service much earlier, on 4 December 1939, prey to war-time economy measures. Interestingly, the track remained in situ, and the Stephenson Locomotive Society was able to run a 'last special' as late as 23 March, 1957. Bromshall Junction had, however, long been severed and the special had to stop short of the junction.

Next to go was the southern end of the Longton, Adderley Green & Bucknall Railway, on 23 December 1963, with the closure of Park Hall Colliery. The other end of this line, which had been severed as a through route as long ago as January 1895, lasted until 6 July 1964, although its last traffic (for Mossfield Colliery) had ceased when that pit closed in May the previous year. The Tutbury-Burton passenger service, 'The Tutbury Jenny', latterly a push-pull operation, ceased on 13 June 1960, and the section of line between Marston Junction and Dove Junction fell out of use from 20 October 1966. This left the old GN route intact between Dove Junction and Eggington Junction, and on to Burton via

Cheadle station on 22 May 1958, with the 4.15pm ex-Macclesfield having just arrived behind Stoke 2-6-4T No.42585. The Cheadle branch was never worked as a traditional branch line, and the trains that served it were always extensions of workings over other lines, notably the Potteries Loop. This would be the case here, the train having travelled via the Loop, and it would return the same way. (W. A. Camwell)

the former NSR. This too soon closed, however, together with the GNR line to Derby, both from 6 May 1968. The short section between Stretton Junction and Burton NS Junction had already closed, on 4 April 1966, and thereafter all traffic used either the Hawkins Lane line, or the former LNWR route to Shrobnall Junction.

Although the Churnet Valley line lost its through passenger services on 7 November 1960, it was 4 January 1965 before the section between Oakamoor and Uttoxeter closed – Leek to North Rode having gone earlier, on 15 June 1964. This left the section between Leek and Oakamoor open, reached on the direct line from Stoke. The Cheadle Railway

was the only surviving branch; it lost its passenger service on 17 June 1963 but goods, and latterly sand, survived until 1988. Surprisingly, and for no obvious reason, much of the track remains in situ. This interesting line had a very troublesome tunnel, almost one mile long, which over the years suffered a series of collapses in the lining. This culminated in a very serious fall on 2 November 1918, when 400ft. of roof collapsed at the Cheadle end. Despite repairs, troubles persisted and the LMS was forced to build a diversion line, 2 miles 509 yards long, to by-pass the tunnel to its south, and this opened 26 November, 1933.

Above. **Summer down holiday special passing Leigh (between Uttoxeter and Stoke) on 19 August 1961, with Burton-on-Trent allocated 'Crab' No.42824. This was one of five members of the class fitted in 1953 with Reidinger rotary poppet valve gear, all five having previously been fitted with Lentz rotary poppet valve gear in 1931 – for many years they were all allocated to Burton. This train has special reporting number 1T11; the T was the London Midland Region code for special passenger trains and at least one of the coaches on this train is labelled from Yarmouth. This train would be carrying returning Potteries holidaymakers, as this was the last weekend of the area's 'Wakes Fortnight'. Notice the gas lamps in their glass cases on the platform. (Michael Mensing)**

Down 16.15 Derby to Crewe train, having just passed Bromshall Junction on 19 August 1961. The train, unusually, consists of two three car BRCW DMU sets (Later Class 104), a more usual formation being one three car set only. Doubtless this would be a method of working a unit back to either Stoke or Crewe. Notice the tall Bromshall Junction signal box in the background, one of the tallest on the NSR; just in front of it can be seen the formation where the Stafford & Uttoxeter branch left the main line. The bracket post for the junction home signal can still be seen on for the signal post just beyond the signal box. (Michael Mensing)

Bromshall level crossing was the box north of the junction, where the B5027 Uttoxeter to Stone road crossed the line, and this view looking north is dated 28 March 1965 – not long before the box closed and the crossing was converted to automatic half barriers. This is an LMS style replacement box, dating from the early War years when an ROF factory was established here. Connection was made in 1942, not only with the main line but with another one controlled by the Junction box on the Stafford & Uttoxeter line. After closure of this box on 21 May 1967, the junction with the ROF Siding was controlled by a ground frame released from Hockley Crossing box at Uttoxeter, as Bromshall Junction box had already been abolished by this date. The ROF closed in December 1968 and the site has since been cleared. Whilst the ROF was known as Bramshall, the NSR always referred to this locality as Bromshall. However, on closure of the crossing box, it 'officially' became Bramshall. (FW Shuttleworth)

Up goods approaching Tutbury Crossing on 30 March 1968 hauled by EE Type 4 D341 and passing the site of Tutbury Station – then only recently demolished. This station closed, along with many others on the route, on 7 November 1966. JC Staton's Tutbury Mill was served from here; the private siding connection is just visible on the extreme left in front of the loading dock. In the right distance can be seen Tutbury Yard signal box. The station here reopened on 3 April 1989 as Tutbury & Hatton, which better describes its location at Hatton; it's a good ¼ mile from Tutbury. It is a completely new station, the old one having been totally demolished in the interim. (Allan C Baker)

RCTS 'St George' railtour on 23 April 1966, seen here hauled by 'Crab' 2-6-0 No 42727 of Birkenhead approaching the sidings at Ettiley Heath, between Sandbach and Hassell Green, a view looking towards Sandbach. The signal is the Elton Crossing Down distant. This tour had started at Nuneaton, and travelled via Walsall, Wednesbury, Wolverhampton, Shrewsbury, Wellington, Market Drayton, Crewe, the Over & Walton Branch, Northwich, Middlewich, Sandbach, Stoke, Burton-on-Trent, and back to Nuneaton. Of the 240 miles travelled, over half had either lost, or never had a passenger service. The 'Crab' came on the train at Crewe. (Michael Mensing)

Another view of an up train arriving at Kidsgrove from Crewe, this time a mixed freight with Class 4 tank No.42590, another Stoke engine, in charge. The date is 26 September 1960 again, and notice the two ex-locomotive tenders behind the engine, used for carrying sludge from water softening plants. The line from Alsager was at a ruling grade of 1 in 100, and loaded trains were often banked. Indeed when open, Alsager shed had a regular banking diagram. However, this train appears to have ascended unaided. Notice to the left the platform edge of the former Down Crewe line bay, used for Audley and Sandbach line trains, and the gas lighting. The 'Car 3 Stop' board on one of the posts was to assist DMU drivers, as unlike drivers of steam locomotives it was not so easy to look back.(Michael Mensing)

CHAPTER FOUR
CREWE AND SANDBACH LINES

The line from Kidsgrove (or Harecastle as the NSR called it) to Crewe, eight miles 30 chains, opened on 9 October 1848, at the same time as the 'main line' to Congleton. Intermediate stations were provided at Alsager and Radway Green & Barthomley, and it was double track throughout. The line joined the LNWR at Crewe North Stafford Junction, south of Crewe station.

The powers to build the Lawton to Sandbach line were included in the same original NSR Act which authorised the Crewe line. The Sandbach line, however, was not completed for some time, until 21 January 1852. It was six miles 40 chains long, of which two thirds or so was single track. There was no junction with the LNW at Sandbach, the line terminating at the NSR's own station at Wheelock – goods traffic was handled at Ettiley Heath, a short distance east of Wheelock. Ettiley Heath was at first goods only, but passenger traffic began on 3 July 1893. A junction with the LNWR at Sandbach, facing Stockport, had eventually been provided, in January 1886; its purpose was the passage of goods and mineral traffic destined for the LNWR line beyond Sandbach to Middlewich to Northwich, particularly the Brunner Mond (later ICI) factories located there. Other than this traffic, the line continued to operate much as it had done in the first days; passenger services still terminated at the NSR Wheelock station, until their early demise, and NSR trains never provided a connection with the LNWR (and later LMS trains) at Sandbach (LNW) station. Local goods traffic was worked only as far as Ettiley Heath.

The Sandbach line junction with the LNW's Manchester route lay just south of Sandbach LNW station, on the former Manchester & Birmingham line. This had opened between Manchester and Crewe (where it joined the GJR) in sections as follows: Manchester-Stockport 4 June 1840; Stockport-Sandbach 10 May 1842; Sandbach-Crewe 10 August 1842.

The Sandbach branch never generated much passenger traffic, and was one of the first of the NSR lines to lose its passenger service, on 28 July 1930. There were intermediate stations at Lawton, Hassall Green and the terminus at Wheelock & Sandbach, almost one mile from Sandbach itself. Despite the early loss of the passenger service, the line remained an important goods link with the Brunner Mond (later ICI) and other chemical industries at both Northwich and nearby Willington. There was a busy flow of minerals and chemicals to and from the Potteries and Northwich, as well as other flows heading south and routed this way in order to miss Crewe. There was a level crossing at Lawton, replaced by half barriers on 20 September 1964, and a passing loop at Hassall Green. The section from Wheelock to Hassall Green had been doubled from 18 April 1893, but the whole line was singled (with a loop at Hassall Green) in the early part of the last War.

It is interesting to note that, from September 1969 until it closed, only Up trains traversed the Sandbach route, all Down traffic going via Crewe. By this time, the only traffic was to and from the ICI complex at Northwich, and southbound loaded trains travelled via Middlewich, Sandbach and this branch. Down trains, by contrast, were routed to the exchange sidings at Hartford, on the West Coast Main Line north of Winsford, and thus went via Crewe and the West Coast Main Line. ICI had its own private railway from Hartford to Northwich.

Sandbach to Lawton closed completely on 3 January 1971, but Kidsgrove-Crewe remains open, though the section between Barthomley, just north of Radway Green and Crewe North Stafford Sidings, is now single track. This section was singled from 25 July 1985, having been temporarily closed beyond Alsager on 2 June 1985, during the extensive Crewe remodelling work. A bus service bridged the gap in the meantime. This saved the cost of relaying both Up and Down tracks.

Kidsgrove Central Junction (known as Harecastle Junction until 2 October 1944) looking south on 20 September 1960. The two three car BRCW DMUs are working the 15.30 Stoke to Manchester Piccadilly and are carrying the local B4 headcode (note the destination London Road, despite the station at Manchester having already changed its name to Piccadilly). The Crewe lines are in the foreground, the view looks south and the train has just emerged from the northernmost, and shortest of the three Harecastle tunnels, later to be opened out to form a cutting. Just behind the first vehicle can be seen the retaining wall of the Trent & Mersey Canal and on top of this the trackbed of the old industrial line connecting Kidsgrove Goods Yard with the Bath Pool area. This was used by the various owners of the collieries, iron works, forges and foundries at Birchenwood, to gain access to parts of their estate. Note too, the later design of McKenzie & Holland signal box. (Michael Mensing)

Alsager East Junction on 16 April 1967, looking south. The lines on the extreme right and before the row of wagons (the latter awaiting attention at Settle Speakman's adjacent wagon works, the roof of which can just be discerned) are the Audley lines, still in situ and fully signalled, although only used for serving the yard and wagon works. Notice the junction bracket signal centre right, still has the Audley line Home signal, with the Alsager Yard Up Audley line distant - the signal on the extreme right is the Alsager Yard Up Audley line home. Amazing this signalling should still survive so long after the Audley line closed. (Allan C Baker)

Alsager East Junction, looking north on 16 June 1967. This was during the period after the Harecastle Tunnel Diversion had been opened, when it was found that up steam hauled goods trains, climbing the 1 in 80 of the new line as it left Kidsgrove, had an unfortunate habit of tripping the circuit breakers controlling the overhead line current. This was on account of the heavy exhaust reverberating off the tunnel roof, and upsetting the contact wire. So, EE Type 4s were kept at Alsager East Junction to assist all steam hauled freights, of which there were still many, between Alsager East Junction, or Lawton Junction or Kidsgrove itself (if the trains were off the Manchester line) and right through to Bradwell Sidings at Longport. They then ran back light to Alsager to await another assignment. This practice came into force on 2 January 1967, and remained until through working of steam trains ceased on the closure of Stoke shed, in August 1967. Here are two of the diesels, in a view looking north; D255 on the right is coupled to a Class 5, and the pair are propelling back on to their train, while the other Type 4 has just arrived back from Bradwell Sidings, and is waiting to cross over and await another train to assist. On the extreme left can be seen the disused coaling stage of Alsager shed, and the extreme left-hand track, is the former Up Audley line. (Dave Donkin)

Alsager Yard signal box on 16 April 1967; when the Audley line was open, this was a block post. Special arrangements existed after Diglake signal box closed and the block section was a long one, all the way to Leycett. As the gradient was an almost steady 1 in 50 for two miles to Diglake, a bank engine could detach there and return to Alsager without going through the section to Leycett, or stay at Diglake while the train engine did some shunting, if this was the case. Interestingly, both the special bank engine key, and the main token had to be carried by the bank engine, and the main token was only to be passed to the driver of the train engine, as the bank engine left to run light back to Alsager Yard. The box dates from September 1891, and replaced an earlier one. (Allan C Baker)

Alsager station and signal box on 16 April 1967, looking south. The signal box, station house, and station buildings are all typical of early NSR practice. Notice the wooden toilet buildings way down the up, left-hand platform, and the relatively new electric lighting. The signal box here was once much higher, but the original superstructure appears to have been re-used, with a shorter brick base. (Allan C Baker)

Radway Green & Barthomley station, looking north in the early 1960s. Notice NSR station buildings and signal box to right. The road connects the B5077 Alsager to Crewe road with Barthomley, a mile away. This station closed on 7 November 1966; more recently, the line has been singled between Alsager and Crewe. If one took this photograph today the M6 would dominate the background.(Allan C Baker)

Six car BRCW DMU, with the 10.50 Derby to Crewe train passing Barthomley, on Good Friday, 4 April 1958. Notice in background Barthomley signal box, just above the train. This block post dated from 1939; it was a mile and 1,087 yards from Crewe North Stafford Sidings, and split the other-wise long, three miles 1,730 yard section between Crewe and Radway Green. It was a wartime measure, but latterly was only switched in during the busy times at Stoke 'Wakes Fortnight', when a lot of special trains were passing. It closed completely in December 1963. (Michael Mensing)

Hassall Green signal box, looking towards Sandbach on 16 April 1967. There is a passing loop beyond the level crossing. The site of the former second line is to left; the station was located here and closed when passenger services were withdrawn over the branch, on 28 July 1930. (Allan C Baker)

Elton Crossing, 16 April 1967, looking towards the junction with the former LNWR at Sandbach. The factory on the right is the famous Foden Motor Works, and the site of the former siding connection can just be made out to the right of the siding. Notice the electric token instrument in the signal box, for the section Elton Crossing to Hassell Green. Sandbach station (actually always called Sandbach & Wheelock, as it was at the latter place) was located between Ettiley Heath and Hassell Green, and was slightly better placed to serve the needs of the town than the LNWR one, which was at Elworth, about a mile to the north. (Allan C Baker)

Up Loop Line coal train approaching Etruria Junction on the 1 in 40 down grade in 1947, showing Etruria Gasworks to the left and, in front of it, some of the cottages of Etruria village. Etruria Station Goods Offices can be seen by the overbridge to the right, taking the main Hanley to Newcastle road over the railway, and just left of the signal (the Etruria Junction down Loop advanced starter). The locomotive is Stoke's Fowler Class 4 tank No.2344 (later BR No 42344). (EJD Warrillow Collection; Keele University Library)

The 1.55pm Manchester to Stoke train, consisting of a three car BRCW DMU, leaving Hanley for Stoke on 28 September 1963. Hanley Station can be seen in the cutting behind the bridge, which carried the Hanley to Newcastle road over the railway. It will be observed that the main station buildings were not at platform level but, due to the confined surroundings, at street level. They can be seen to the right above the bridge. The sharp curve here, brought about when the Hanley Branch was extended to form part of the Loop Line in July 1865, severely restricted the types of locomotive and coaches that could traverse the line – BR Mark 1 coaches for example, were barred. (Michael Mensing)

CHAPTER FIVE
THE LOOP LINE

The most famous of all the NSR branch lines is without doubt the Potteries Loop, immortalised, like no other, in the writings of Arnold Bennett. Seven miles and twenty-four chains of undulating, curving and steeply graded line, it served the Pottery towns of Hanley, Burslem – the Mother town – and Tunstall, as well as the villages of Cobridge, Pitts Hill, Newchapel & Goldenhill. It formed a loop between the main line at Etruria, north of Stoke, and Kidsgrove where it joined the main line again. As all these towns and villages stood on higher ground than the main line, which followed the Chatterley Valley, the gradients were severe. The line also served many mineral workings, including collieries at Hanley Deep Pit, Sneyd, Chatterley Whitfield and Birchenwood – there was also the iron and steel works at Etruria, always known locally as Shelton Bar, and in earlier days an ironworks at Birchenwood.

First moves came as early as 1850, when a branch was built from Etruria to serve Earl Granville's iron works at Shelton. This was the very first of many NSR branches built over the following years, and it was extended to Hanley, opening to passengers on 13 July 1864. A after a lapse of some time, it was gradually extended in sections thus:-

Hanley-Burslem 1November 1873
Burslem-Tunstall 1 December 1873
Tunstall-Newchapel & Goldenhill 1 October 1874

Newchapel & Goldenhill-Kidsgrove 15 November 1875

The last section took a long time, for not only did the line have to descend from a considerable height, it also had to pass through an existing iron and steel works at Birchenwood, largely in a deep cutting, but partly in a short 88 yard tunnel.

There were two branches, Tunstall Upper and Lower, which had originally been projected as one, running from Longport, via Tunstall to Newfields, north of Tunstall. Indeed, construction had commenced when the Loop Line was conceived. As a result, they had to be modified to suit, and were thus split into two separate lines. Consequently the Lower Branch (officially the Spur Line, but generally referred to as the Pinnox Branch) ran for one mile and eight chains from Longport – on the main line – to Tunstall, where it joined the Loop. It opened on 1 June 1875. Later, a connection was made at about its mid-point with the Whitfield & Pinnox Mineral Railway, a private line opened in 1878 and joining this part of Tunstall with Chatterley Whitfield Colliery, in the Biddulph Valley. Coal from this pit, destined for shipment north via Birkenhead or Liverpool, could then avoid the otherwise circuitous route via Stoke, and the higher NSR haulage rates associated with it.

The Upper Branch, 61 chains long and generally known as the Newfields Branch, opened 1 October 1874. As the earlier projected route was bisected by

the Loop, this branch had perforce, in view of the gradients, to make an awkward zig-zag junction at what became Newfields Junction, north of Tunstall. The branches were goods and mineral only, although the Pinnox Branch was always passed for passenger traffic, and served on occasion for diversionary purposes. Both were single track, while the Loop, after it was extended beyond Hanley, was double.

In its heyday the Loop was very busy (there was a fifteen minute interval passenger service to Tunstall at peak times) but it fell foul, first of the electric tramcar, and later the motor bus. Goods and mineral traffic was heavy too, with coal from Sneyd and Hanley Deep Pit Collieries generally using the Pinnox Branch. To serve the Birchenwood complex at Kidsgrove, a 'Third Line' was built from Kidsgrove Junction to 'The Summit', north of Newchapel & Goldenhill, thus keeping the mineral traffic off the Loop proper.

Some through traffic also traversed the Loop Line, with a proportion of the North Stafford's Macclesfield and Congleton trains using this route rather then the main line. Later, in LMS and BR days, some of the through Manchester to Stoke and Birmingham trains went this way.

With its severe gradients, one and a half miles of 1 in 40 climbing out of Kidsgrove, and a mile or so of not much less from Etruria, the line was always difficult to work. When diversions of main

An up train consisting of a BRCW three car DMU, forming a service to Derby but diverted over the Loop due to engineering works on the main line. It is passing Cobridge Station in about 1960. The view looks north, the chimney in the distance marking the site of Sneyd Colliery at Burslem. Diesel railcars, later known as Diesel Multiple Units (DMUs), were introduced onto the local services from 16 September 1957 between Crewe and Derby, and on 3 March the following year between Manchester and Birmingham, together with most of the other shorter distance local services. A new depot was built at Cockshute Sidings, by Newcastle Junction, to maintain the units and this opened in October 1957. All the original units allocated except for one parcels vehicle, were of this BRCW type. They were used in three or six car formations, although there were a small number of twin car units. (Authors Collection)

Down Wedgwood Pottery Factory workers' train calling at Cobridge on a summer evening in 1960. This was one of the last steam hauled passenger trains in the district, and dates from the wartime opening of the new Wedgwood factory at Barlaston south of Stoke, which replaced the original and historic facilities at Etruria. This train started from Stone at 5.9pm and called at Wedgwood Halt from 5.17pm to 5.22pm, then ran all stations to Newchapel & Goldenhill where it arrived at six o'clock. It then returned empty stock to Stoke Cockshute Sidings and was always a regular Stoke Class 4F duty – this one is No.44246. It always puzzled me why they did not use a Class 4 tank on this job, of which Stoke had plenty. (LA Dutton)

line trains took place, assisting engines often had to be provided, and this made life even more difficult, especially if it was at short notice. On the Pinnox Branch, there was a section as steep as 1 in 37. Because of this, and the sharp curves, a number of NSR engines were specially designed with this line in mind, and there were always severe restrictions as to what locomotives and rolling stock could be used. For example, the BR standard Mk1 rolling stock would not pass through the platforms at Hanley, and the ex-LMS Class 5 was the largest engine that could be used on the route.

Closure came in stages, and as the local collieries and other industries contracted, so did the traffic. First to close

For a number of years after all the old NSR engines had been scrapped, Stoke had a small allocation of ex-LNWR 'Cauliflower' 0-6-0s, specifically for working the Newfields branch. This short 61 chain branch left the Loop by a zig-zag junction just north of Tunstall to serve a wharf alongside the main Kidsgrove to Tunstall road at Sandyford. The awkward junction arrangements were necessary because the branch was originally part of a projected through route from Longport; having been partly constructed when it was decided to build the Loop, the levels were wrong for a conventional junction layout. In view of weight restrictions on the line only very light engines could be used, and it closed on 3 August 1959. Here is No 58382 arriving at Tunstall with the Down 'Newfields Shunt', on 29 June 1953. (FW Shuttleworth)

The 'Newfields Shunt' shunting at the south end of the sidings at Newchapel & Goldenhill, prior to running back to Newfield Junction and propelling up the branch. It was the normal arrangement to do the shunting here as there were few facilities at either the junction or Newfields itself, so that the train formation was correct before ascending the branch. Here is No.53832 again on 29 June 1953. (FW Shuttleworth)

was the Newfields Branch, which had boasted but one local trip working on weekdays for years, and this ceased on 3 August 1959. The Pinnox Branch followed on 17 February 1964, its main reason in life by this date being the coal traffic from Chatterley Whitfield Colliery, and this ceased on closure of the private Whitfield & Pinnox Mineral Railway. Thereafter, traffic to and from this colliery passed via a new connection with the Biddulph Valley line at Chell. The Loop itself lost its local passenger services, together with other remaining branch lines in the area, on 2 March 1964. However, it was retained as a through route, for diversionary purposes

while the electrification works were under way on the main line, and was occasionally used as such. However, the section beyond Waterloo Road was closed completely on 3 January 1966, though the 'Third Line' was still in use at the Kidsgrove end to serve the Birchenwood Coking Plant. The section from Etruria to Waterloo Road was retained to serve Walkers Oil Refinery, but when traffic ceased there on 31 July 1969, this too closed.

The 'Third Line' had a new lease of life when local open-cast coal working commenced in the Newchapel & Goldenhill district, and a new rapid loading bunker was built in 1970, over the

line at Park Farm, just north of the old station. Fortunately, the track was still in situ here and with some slewing, connection was made with the 'Third Line', so that the best of the remaining track could be used. The Birchenwood Coking Plant closed in 1973, with the last traffic passing on 5 July that year, and the Park Farm operations finished in January 1976. Official closure of this, the Third Line, and a section of the Loop proper beyond Birchenwood Summit Junction, came on 25 August 1976 but as we have seen, there would have been little or no traffic since the previous January.

The Loop Line climbs out of Kidsgrove by a continuous almost one and a half miles of 1 in 40, bisecting the Birchenwood site in a cutting and short tunnel. There were formerly collieries and ironworks here, but latterly only a coking plant survived, albeit a large one. This view taken on 2 May 1958 looks south, up the incline, and towards Newchapel & Goldenhill. The bunkers of the coking ovens can be seen to the right and the coke loading bunker to the left. One of the two rail connections to the works can just be seen leaving the right-hand track by the tunnel mouth. It appears to climb on the embankment into the works, but is actually almost level. By this time the right-hand track was only used for Birchenwood traffic though it was always, and indeed 'officially', referred to as 'The Third Line'. The Loop had been double track, but was singled on 13 May 1907, a fact hardly discernible from this picture due to subsequent slips of the cutting sides and building of the retaining wall. However, the tunnel has room for three tracks through it and I believe this was the only three track tunnel ever built in this country. The signal is the Kidsgrove Liverpool Road Junction, down distant. (Late Dr JR Hollick)

Harts Hill signal box, looking towards Stoke in 1959. This was the first block post on the line, located where the double track section became single for the two tunnels between here and Newcastle – the superstructure of this box was unusual for the North Stafford; notice the ornamental barge boards. There used to be a halt here, Harts Hill & Basford, opened 1 May 1905 when the railmotors were introduced. It closed on 20 September 1926. The box dates from the April 1885, doubling of the line from Newcastle Junction as far as this point. The line here is climbing towards Newcastle at 1 in 102. (Authors Collection)

Newcastle station looking towards Stoke on 25 April 1964 – note the unusual position of the signal box on the down side platform. The booking hall was on the road bridge which took the main Newcastle to Hanley road over the railway. Note also the 'P 10/1956' paint date on the up platform awning. The section Newcastle Junction to Brampton Sidings closed to all traffic 8 March 1966, with the remaining section served by the relatively new Chord Line at Madeley, connecting the branch with the ex-LNWR West Coast Main Line. (Collection MG Fell)

CHAPTER SIX
A LINE INTO SHROPSHIRE

The NSR route from Stoke to the Shropshire market town of Market Drayton has its foundations in the earliest of the company's Acts of Incorporation. One of the three original Acts of 1846, 'The NSR Pottery Line Act', as well as authorising Macclesfield to Colwich, included a branch to Silverdale via Newcastle. No progress was made, however, and as a result Ralph Sneyd, a prominent local landowner of Sneyd Hall, granted powers for Francis Stanier (lessee of much of Sneyd's mineral bearing property around Silverdale) to build a railway from the mines and ironworks at Silverdale, to Newcastle-under-Lyme, at a place called Pool Dam, west of the town.

This line, the Silverdale & Newcastle Railway (2 miles 28 chains long) was a private concern, built without statutory powers and opened some time in 1849-50. In this way Stanier was able to move his coal and other minerals into Newcastle for sale. Meantime, doubtless prompted into action by this activity, the NSR built its own line, commencing sixteen chains north of Stoke (at what became Newcastle Junction) via two tunnels, 96 and 650 yards long, under a 500ft. ridge of high ground for the 1¼ miles to Newcastle.

Even so, the ruling grade was 1 in 102. The line continued onwards a further mile to a junction with Sneyd's line, at what became Knutton Junction. Contiguous with the building of this line was a branch to Apedale, leaving the main route at what became Apedale Junction, 970 yards from Newcastle. This was to serve Richard-Edensor Heathcote's Apedale Colliery and Ironworks, and was 1 mile 4 furlongs long. Included in the agreement to build the line beyond Newcastle was the use of part of the course of the Newcastle-under-Lyme Junction Canal, between Newcastle itself the site of the later Brampton Crossing. This canal had opened in 1799, to extend an earlier canal ('Gresley's Canal', itself opened in 1776) running between Apedale Ironworks and the Liverpool Road. Gresley's daughter had married Heathcote, hence the latter became owner of the Apedale Estate. At the later site of Brampton Crossing, the canal turned north and then north-west, to join Gresley's Canal, north of its terminus and alongside the London to Carlisle turnpike road – Liverpool Road – north of Newcastle town itself. Part of this southern stub of the canal had to be abandoned too, for the

new railway went under its alignment almost at its terminus basin. A section of the Junction Canal remained, however, from the Gresley Canal end, to serve a cotton factory at Cross Heath, and coal was brought there by canal boat from the Apedale Collieries for some years more. Newcastle Junction to Knutton Junction opened on 6 September 1852, with passenger traffic commencing between Stoke and Newcastle on the same day. An intermediate halt, Hartshill and Basford, situated just south of the tunnels, opened much later, on 1 May 1905. The Apedale Branch opened 11 July, 1853.

To enable Sneyd's line to be used for passengers between Knutton Junction and Silverdale, an Act of Parliament was necessary, and this was duly obtained in March 1859; by a later Act of 1860 powers were granted to the NSR to lease the line. Sneyd, and his lessees, nevertheless retained powers to use the line for their own trains, and indeed continued to exercise them. In May 1863 passenger services commenced between Newcastle and Silverdale. Meanwhile, Sneyd's line at Pool Dam had been extended a meagre half mile, by the grandiosely titled Newcastle-under-Lyme

Newcastle Goods Yard, from the road overbridge looking south. This is the site of the former Newcastle-under-Lyme Junction Canal, converted to a railway as a part of the scheme to give railway access to Apedale and Silverdale. The road to the left is Water Street, so named for this reason. Note the NSR Goods Shed and the capstans used for shunting. The road overbridge here gave extremely restricted clearance, belying its parentage, and by the time this photograph was taken on 4 May 1956, there were no locomotives of a height low enough to pass under it – hence the capstans for moving the wagons. In NSR days only the much rebuilt 0-6-0 saddle tanks Nos.58 and 59 (later 58A and 59A in the duplicate list) could negotiate this bridge, which had a clearance of 11ft.8in. These two were built by Hudswell Clarke & Rogers of Leeds in 1866, and rebuilt extensively at Stoke in 1880-81, so much so that to all intents and purposes they were 'accountants' rebuilds. They were scrapped in 1927 and 1930 respectively, as LMS Nos.1600-1601. (Late Dr JR Hollick)

Canal Extension Railway; it opened some time in 1854, and thus made connection with the Newcastle-under-Lyme Canal at Stubbs Gate. This canal had opened in 1800, and ran four miles from a junction with the Trent & Mersey Canal in Stoke, to Stubbs Gate in Newcastle.

The route onward to Market Drayton, 12 miles 37 chains, was authorised by an Act of 1864 and, double track throughout, opened to both goods and passenger traffic on 1 February 1870, with intermediate stations at Keele, Madeley Road, Pipe Gate and Norton in Hales. At Market Drayton junction was made with the GWR line from Nantwich to Wellington, which had opened in two sections. (See Audley Line notes, Chapter Six.) An engine shed was established at Market Drayton, the NSR, taking over an earlier building of Great Western origin.

Relations with the GW were cordial, and not only did the NSR enjoy running powers over its line southward to Hodnet and for all traffic, but also to Wellington, if only for merchandise. The GWR enjoyed similar powers for merchandise traffic all the way to Stoke, and this brought copper capped chimneys to the city every day, with a single through working between Shrewsbury and Stoke. A Dean 0-6-0 goods engine was the usual motive power in later NSR and LMS days.

Passenger traffic over the line suffered in the post-war period, along with all branch lines, and services were withdrawn west of Silverdale on and from 7 May 1956. For a few years afterwards

passenger excursion trains ran from Stoke-on-Trent for the annual Battle of Britain commemorative celebrations at Tern Hill aerodrome – Tern Hill was the first station south of Market Drayton on the Wellington line. Passenger trains survived between Stoke and Silverdale, albeit as a very sparse service, until 28 March 1964, the same date the Loop Line and Cheadle Branch services were withdrawn.

Provision was made in the 1864 Act for a curve at Madeley Road, facing Market Drayton, to connect with the Down Crewe line of the LNWR main line, but despite completion of the earthworks, the track was never laid. However, many years later, with the modernising of Basford Hall Marshalling Yard at Crewe and construction of a new Freight Concentration Depot at Stoke, the decision was taken to lay track on what became known as the Madeley Chord, and route Stoke-Crewe traffic this way – it opened 18 June 1962. This had the added advantage of freeing the former NS main line north of Stoke of much traffic, while electrification work was under way. A new signal box was opened at Madeley Road, and part of the erstwhile Down line was reinstated to form a loop. It had been singled from 7 October 1934. This re-routing of traffic, incidentally, saw the virtual end of Alsager as a marshalling point, and the closure of the engine shed, along with the Audley line.

The new flow of traffic was nevertheless short-lived and once the electrification works were over, with the continu-

ing gradual decline in freight, the line was closed as a through route on and from 8 March 1966. The track was quickly lifted between Newcastle Junction and Brampton Sidings, but was left in place between Madeley Chord and Market Drayton for a couple of years. Indeed, this section was not officially closed until 9 January 1967. It was occasionally used for out of season storage of wagons – coal wagons in the summer months, and sugar beet vans out of the beet season. Thereafter, the section between Madeley Chord and Brampton Sidings, together with part of the Apedale Branch, were served from Crewe, rather than Stoke, and in the main for traffic to and from Holditch and Silverdale Collieries.

The Pool Dam branch closed 7 October 1967 and the Apedale Branch with the closure of Holditch Colliery in August 1989, along with the line south of Silverdale to Apedale Junction and Brampton Sidings. The section Madeley Chord-Silverdale remained open for some years, and despite the varying fortunes of Silverdale Colliery in recent times, coal traffic continued to flow, usually north from Madeley to Crewe, until Silverdale too, closed, on the last day of 1998. The modern BR-built Madeley Chord signal box closed 22 August 1971, and operations were transferred to the main line box at Madeley, interestingly enough still one of LNWR origin. With the closure of Silverdale Colliery this section of track, presumably, will close too – the last remnant of a line into Shropshire.

A train of Holditch Colliery coal heads west at Knutton, seen here passing Ketleys Siding on 23 January 1965. The locomotive is 8F 2-8-0 No.48600 of Stoke and the train, possibly destined for Ironbridge Power Station, would be heading for Market Drayton and Wellington. The line on the right is a goods loop to serve the Pool Dam branch, which can be seen curving away to the right, almost opposite the Apedale Junction up distant. (MG Fell)

Knutton looking west towards Newcastle on 4 April 1956, with a train hauled by a tender first 4F 0-6-0, having just come off the Pool Dam branch. To the right are the former loading banks and disused siding cutting. This was where coal and ironstone was brought by road from nearby workings for transhipment into railway wagons. The junction with the Pool Dam branch was controlled by Ketley's Siding signal box, just off the picture to the left, but formerly there was another box just beyond the train, Knutton Junction. The engine would shortly run round its train, before setting off for Stoke. (Late Dr JR Hollick)

Standard Class 2 2-6-0 No.78056 of Stoke shed with a brake van special at Pool Dam, on the Silverdale & Newcastle-under-Lyme Railway, on 25 April 1964. This train also traversed the Loop, Chesterton and Apedale branches. There was a wharf here and the branch continued towards Newcastle (the Newcastle-under-Lyme Canal Extension Railway, built to connect the Silverdale & Newcastle-under-Lyme Railway with the Newcastle-under-Lyme Canal at its terminus, and opened in 1854) to serve the Gas Works and a structural steel works, together with another public wharf. (Late Dr JR Hollick)

Up short goods train approaching Ketley's Siding on 9 August 1966, with Ivatt Class 2 No.43024 of Crewe South shed, heading towards Brampton Sidings. By this date the line between Stoke Newcastle Junction and Brampton Sidings had closed, and the remainder of the route was served from Crewe via Madeley Chord. This train of empty mineral wagons was destined for scrap dealers Hampton's, whose yard was at Brampton Sidings. From there they despatched scrap by rail. The signal is the Ketley's Siding up home – notice the Tileries on the right, formerly rail served and owned by J H Ketley – hence the name of the signal box. Until about the time of the First World War the box had been known as Gordon's Siding, after an earlier owner of works hereabouts. (Allan C Baker)

Apedale Junction, looking west towards Newcastle on 29 April 1967, and showing Class 8F 2-8-0 No.48375 of Crewe South, coming off the Apedale branch with a coal train from Holditch Colliery. The train would then run to Brampton Sidings, where the engine would run round, before proceeding to Madeley Chord and thence to Crewe Sorting Sidings. Holditch Colliery, incidentally, which dated from just after the First World War, closed in July 1989. Thereafter, the remains of the Market Drayton line were confined to the section between Madeley Chord and Silverdale. The pit at Holditch was usually known locally as Brymbo, after its original owners, The Brymbo Steel Company of Wrexham, but in 1930 it passed to the ownership of the local Shelton Iron Steel & Coal Company. The box closed 24 September 1967 on introduction of 'one engine in steam' working beyond Silverdale. (MG Fell)

Another view of the brake van special hauled by 78056, this time at the extreme end of the Apedale branch. The view looks towards Apedale Junction, the engine having already run round its train for the return journey. The branch was retained to this point after the closure of the Apedale Ironworks in 1930, as there were no facilities for engines to run round their trains at Holditch Colliery. This pit was served by a branch from the Apedale line, leaving it at Whitebarn Junction, just south of where the line crossed over the Milehouse to Knutton road. By running round at Apedale the train could be drawn back clear of the level crossing, and then propelled into the colliery yard – it served the additional purpose of reducing the time trains would block the level crossing, fouling the main Market Drayton line during shunting operations. This remained the practice until the Market Drayton line ceased to be a through route. (Late Dr JR Hollick)

Silverdale signal box and level crossing on 10 May 1964, looking towards Market Drayton, with the colliery to the right. The up side station building can just be seen beyond the level crossing, the road onwards to the colliery being a private one. (Allan C Baker)

Class 3F 0-6-0T No.47606, a long time member of the Stoke fleet (at this date shedded at Alsager, however) coming off the Audley branch at Silverdale in April 1961. The Market Drayton and Audley lines ran as parallel single lines from Silverdale to Keele (site of the former Keele Junction). This working is presumed to be empty wagons for either Holditch or Silverdale Colliery, routed via the Audley line from Alsager to avoid having to travel via Stoke. This was the usual practice until the Chord line was opened at Madeley, after which traffic from the north to and from these pits was marshalled at Crewe rather than Alsager, and joined the Market Dayton line at the Chord rather than via the Audley line. This was of course, the death knell of the line as a through route. (MRC Price - collection Basil Juda)

Site of Keele Junction in 1953, with the Market Drayton curving away to the left, and the Audley line to the right. The junction here was removed when both lines were singled on 7 October 1934, and thereafter they ran as two separate single lines to Silverdale. (Late Tony Birch; courtesy Bernard Holland)

CHAPTER SEVEN
THE AUDLEY LINE

The seven and a half mile line from Keele to Alsager was a part of a strategic move by the NSR, and powers for its construction were embodied in its New Works Act of 1864. There were extensive mineral workings in the area but it nevertheless took embryonic schemes aimed at penetrating the Potteries (backed by GWR interests) to galvanise the Knotty into action. The new powers extended the Silverdale & Newcastle Railway from the former place to Market Drayton, where it was to join the Nantwich & Market Drayton Railway, itself opened 20 October 1863. The route there was extended southwards to Wellington, by the Wellington & Drayton Railway, and this line opened on 19 October 1867. Both the Nantwich & Market Drayton Railway and the Wellington & Drayton Railway were operated by the GWR from inception, and were eventually absorbed into that system.

The Audley line ran from a junction with the Silverdale to Market Drayton line at Honeywall, just west of Keele, and by a junction facing west (i.e. to Market Drayton), through Leycett, Halmerend, Audley, Jamage and onwards, due north, to join the Crewe line by a junction at Alsager. The west-facing junction at Honeywall indicated the direction in which it was felt the mineral traffic would flow. This was in deference to the Great Western-inspired interests, one of the

prices paid for their defeat. The Market Drayton line opened to all traffic on 1 February 1870 and the Audley line (for goods and mineral traffic only) a few months later, on 24 July 1870. There was also a direct line from Silverdale to Leycett, joining the Audley line just north of the station there. However, there were difficulties with its construction; it was largely in deep cuttings and there were severe drainage problems and steep gradients – 1 in 17 in places – that meant little use was made of it. Some sources even suggest that the track was never laid, while others say it *was* laid, but the line was never used. In any event, if it was used if was only for a short period of time. Remains of the cuttings existed within living memory, but all has now been just about completely obscured with waste and rubbish tipping.

There were also two branches; the Jamage branch, 54 chains long to serve Jamage Colliery and a second, 25 chains long to serve Diglake and Bignall Hill Collieries. Both opened at the same time as the Audley line itself. As well as these pits, there were collieries at Leycett (Madeley Colliery, which was also connected by private railway to the LNWR main line at Madeley), Halmerend and at Hayes Wood, where connection was made with the Cooper & Craig-owned Podmore Hall Collieries, and later at Merelake, north of Audley, for Rigby's

Bunkers Hill Colliery. The NSR built an engine shed at Alsager in 1890, primarily to serve the needs of the Audley line. However, primitive coaling and watering facilities had existed there almost from the opening of the line, and doubtless engines were left there overnight quite regularly. The new shed had four roads, 160ft. long, a 50ft. turntable and a 34,400 gallon water tank. The goods sidings here not only served the Audley line, but also acted as a re-marshalling point for general goods traffic, in wagon load or part train loads, to and from northern destinations. Such traffic thus avoided the already busy yards further south. This arrangement continued until June 1962. The building of a chord line at Madeley (connecting the West Coast Main Line with the Market Drayton branch) and the opening of a Freight Concentration Depot at Stoke, meant that thereafter traffic was routed via this chord line, and the Market Drayton branch to Stoke. Alsager shed closed at the same time, as did the Audley line. Motive power for local shunting was provided by this shed, as well as the shunting engines for Kidsgrove (Birchenwood) and Chatterley, and banking engines for the main line to Kidsgrove, and the Audley line to Jamage. For management purposes, in LMS and BR days it was a sub-shed of Crewe South, but the engines were largely from the Stoke fleet, carrying

Class 4F 0-6-0 running tender first, light engine and brake back to Stoke, having been engaged on track lifting operations on the Audley line in 1963. The train is leaving Leycett; the site of Madeley Colliery, closed in 1957, was to the left, behind and beyond the houses. This pit provided the last originating traffic on the line, apart from very small amounts of local traffic, although a landsale wharf was maintained at the colliery site, being rail served, for a couple of years after closure. (Late Tony Birch; courtesy Bernard Holland)

Leycett signal box in 1963, looking north along the Audley line after closure of the route. The station site is beyond the level crossing and Madeley Colliery was to the left, the line curving sharply to the left beyond the site of the station to skirt around the high ground in the background. (Late Tony Birch; courtesy Bernard Holland)

Alsager shed plates and remaining allocated there for long periods.

The junction arrangements at Honeywall proved a problem, for in the event most traffic went to or from the Potteries. Powers were accordingly obtained to build an 'East Curve'; this was authorised by an Act of 1880 and opened on 1 October 1881 (the west facing arrange-

ment closed at the same time) but not before passenger traffic had been introduced on the branch. These had commenced the previous year, on 28 June 1880, requiring an awkward run-round arrangement at Honeywall in the interim. The introduction of passenger services, with stations at Leycett, Halmerend, Audley and Alsager Road,

was prompted by the burgeoning mineral wealth of the area, the pit villages growing into towns in their own right.

In 1890 the Midland Coal Coke & Iron Company (MCC&IC) was formed, amalgamating the interests of the Staniers at Apedale with Cooper & Craig at Halmerend, and a private railway was built to connect the two separate estates.

Audley branch track lifting train at Audley itself in 1963, just south of the former station. View looks due west, with Audley village itself on the sky line to the right – Audley Station was actually at Bignall End, some way from the town. The clump of ground to the extreme right marks the site of the filled in shaft of the Boyles Hall pit, ventilation shaft for the nearby former Diglake Colliery. This was in the days when BR did its own track lifting, notice the crane is in BR ownership. (Late Tony Birch; courtesy Bernard Holland)

Madeley Chord, the new BR built signal box commissioned on 18 June 1962, to control the new junction arrangements between the Market Drayton line and the ex-LNWR main line. The connecting spur, which can just be seen in the distance curving away to the left, utilised a formation put in place when the NSR line was originally constructed in 1870, but never used. Running behind the signal box, at about the level of the small hut, can be seen the West Coast main line, and notice even at this late date semaphore signals in use. Behind the photographer was the site of Madeley Road station, closed to passengers by the LMS in July 1931. The junction arrangements here survived and coal from Silverdale Colliery passed this way, but the signal box disappeared and control was from Madeley box on the main line until the colliery closed in December 1998. 4 February 1967. (Allan C Baker)

This served to lessen traffic on the Audley line but not significantly, the real decline setting in after the First World War. There was a terrible disaster at the MCC&IC Minnie Pit at Halmerend on 12 January 1918. It was North Staffordshire's worst, 155 men and boys losing their lives when a firedamp explosion rent the workings. This was the beginning of the end for the Audley coalfield, and output from this and adjacent pits never resumed pre-war proportions.

The MCC&IC went into liquidation during the Depression, and in November 1929 the pits closed, never to reopen. Following this the pit towns and villages declined, becoming almost ghost towns in some cases, and passenger services ceased on the Audley line on 27 April 1931. This was only the third of the former NSR lines to lose its passenger services, though they had been somewhat meagre for a number of years.

The late Dr J.R. Hollick, knowing of the impending closure, took his one and only trip along the line on Saturday 18 April 1931, just days before the closure. According to his notebook he took the 9.02am from Ashbourne where he then lived, and then the 9.51am from Uttoxeter to Stoke, hauled by Fowler 2-6-4T No.2346, with four coaches. At Stoke, Jack caught the 12.20pm to Harecastle via Audley, the branch trains always running between Stoke and Harecastle (later renamed Kidsgrove Central). There was a bay platform there,

alongside the Down side Crewe line platform, where the Audley line trains awaited their return journey. Fittingly, in this case the train was hauled by LMS No.2248, ex-NSR No.156, a new 'L' Class 0-6-2T, built at Stoke in 1908, and withdrawn in 1937. The train consisted of three coaches and Jack records: '*Very steep gradients on the line, many signals have old slot posts with slots filled in. This line is being closed after April 27, 1931. Double throughout, once a triangle at Keele (in fact, the west facing curve closed at the same time as the east facing one opened).*' He changed at Harecastle into the 1.22pm to Stoke, 2-6-4T No.2346 was the engine again, obviously on its way back from Crewe to Derby.

After the passenger service ceased there was little through traffic, not much more than a daily pick-up goods and some through traffic associated with Holditch and Silverdale Collieries, to and from destinations to the north. Madeley Colliery traffic tended to be worked from Stoke, and Jamage traffic from Alsager. From 7 October 1934 the line was singled, with passing loops at Leycett and Diglake Junction, Audley. The Market Drayton line was singled beyond Silverdale at the same time but the two tracks were left in place between Silverdale and Keele, worked as by-directional single lines, the former Up line for Market Drayton, and the former Down for Audley. There was thus no longer any junction at Keele. Jamage Colliery closed

in late 1941, but the washery and screening plant there remained in use to process coal from nearby Rookery Colliery. When this in turn closed in November 1947, so did the Jamage branch (official closure date was 27 December 1947). However, since the 1934 singling of the Audley line, Jamage Junction had closed, and the branch used the former down line, to regain the main line at Diglake (Audley).

Traffic was extremely sparse after this, though there was a brief spate of activity when opencast coal workings were in operation at Audley (Bignall Hill), between 1954 and 1957. Otherwise, there was just an occasional pick-up goods, some traffic to and from Silverdale and Holditch Collieries which was routed from Alsager this way, and the Madeley Colliery traffic at Leycett, all this going to and from Stoke. Madeley Colliery closed on 20 September 1957 but the sidings remained as a coal landsale site, with incoming rail traffic, until May 1959. 'Landsale', where coal was sold direct from wagons to merchants, rather than sent direct to users, was quite common then. The section between Audley and Silverdale closed 18 June 1962, and the Audley and Alsager section earlier on 7 January 1962. These were, however, but paper closures and the last trains would have been run some months earlier.

Pipe Gate Station, looking towards Silverdale on 4 February 1967 and long after closure of the station. Indeed the line itself had officially closed a month earlier, although it had seen almost no traffic since the previous year. The station arrangements were unusual as the booking office and up side buildings were beyond the platform and at rail level. Conversely it was interesting to find a signal box on a platform, as they were more usually located at ground level. Several of the Market Drayton line signal boxes stood on the station platforms, Newcastle and Norton-in-Hales being the same. The bridge takes the line over the A50 Rugeley to Nantwich road. (Allan C Baker)

Betton Moss level crossing, about ¾ mile on the Silverdale side of where the NSR route joined the former Great Western line from Nantwich to Wellington, on 4 February 1967. There was never a station here, but the house is the ex-NSR crossing keeper's house. Beyond the gates are stored box vans, the line being used for wagon storage by this date. The authors A35 van can be seen on the extreme left. (Allan C Baker)

View from Market Drayton Silverdale Junction, where the branch joined the former GW route, and looking towards Silverdale. Notice surviving NSR McKenzie & Holland signals at this late date, 4 February 1967, although the box and junction arrangements were Great Western. The former Great Western route from Nantwich to Wellington was taken out of use on 8 May 1967, having lost its passenger services on 9 September 1963. (Allan C Baker)

Market Drayton Silverdale Junction, looking north towards Nantwich on 4 February 1967. The Brush Type 4 D1718 is running light from the Nantwich direction towards Wellington, the signalman having rapidly put his up home signal to danger behind it. Notice more box vans stored to the right, beyond the locomotive. In all probability these vans would be used for the seasonal sugar beet traffic, there being a sugar factory at Allscott between Wellington and Shrewsbury – if so, the 1966-67 season must have ended rather early. (Allan C Baker)

Berry Hill signal box in 1957, looking north along the Biddulph Valley line to Botteslow Junction, with surviving NSR McKenzie & Holland signals. The box is switched out on this occasion; the colliery is to the right and the empty wagons await their loads. The colliery closed in April 1960 and the box was taken out of use on 15 August 1965. (Author's Collection)

BR/Sulzer Type 2 D5018 proceeding light and approaching the remains of Bucknall & Northwood station on the evening of 21 July 1967. The engine would be heading for one of the line's collieries to bring the last load of the day to Stoke. (Allan C Baker)

CHAPTER EIGHT
THE BIDDULPH VALLEY LINE

Promoted at first as an independent concern, the 'Potteries Biddulph & Congleton Railway', this twelve mile line ran from Stoke Junction to Congleton Upper Junction, where it joined the main line from Kidsgrove to Macclesfield. There was a mile-long branch from Congleton Lower Junction, passing under the main line to serve Brunswick Wharf, and a goods and mineral station at Congleton itself.

A prominent local coal and iron master, Robert Heath, was instrumental in the line's promotion, as he had interests at Ford Green, Bradley, Brindley Ford and Black Bull, as well as other places in the locality. There were also other developing mineral workings along the proposed route. The line opened on 3 August 1859, to meet the Parliamentary time limit, although it was by no means complete, and it was 28 August the following year before much traffic passed. Passenger services commenced on 1 June 1864.

There were a number of branches, NSR and industrial, as well as a line from Milton Junction which served the market town of Leek directly from the Potteries. This opened on 1 November 1867, joining the Churnet Valley line south of Leek at Leek Brook Junction (formerly Cheddleton). Then came the 'Longton, Adderley Green & Bucknall Railway' (LAG&BR), another independent concern, and one which remained so for a number of years, though it was always operated by the NSR. It was projected as a through route, leaving the Biddulph Valley line at Botteslow Junction, one mile and 55 chains from Stoke Junction, and was three miles and 54 chains long, single track, forming a loop by joining the Stoke to Derby and Burton line at Millfield Junction, Normacot. As the junction there faced Stoke, were it not for Stoke Junction facing north, the loop would have been a continuous one. The Act of Parliament by which it was constructed dated from 16 July 1866 but the line was a long time in opening; not until 24 September 1875 in fact and this despite an extension of time Act being necessary. This, it should be pointed out, only extended the time for completion until 27 June 1874.

There were two branches authorised by the LAG&BR Act, a short one of 37 chains from Hulme Valley Junction (just over two miles from Botteslow) to serve Adderley Green Sidings and Hulme Colliery and another, only 55½ chains, to Fenton Culvert, which in the end was never built.

The line was steeply graded, leaving Botteslow by a continuous average grade of 1 in 50, and for over two miles. This was however, in favour of loaded trains from the line's collieries. As well as Hulme Colliery, the line served the two Mossfield Collieries, Old and New, Adderley Green, Park Hall and Ubberley Collieries, and there were a number of

other smaller workings including Lawn and Brookhouse. Ubberley Colliery was later taken over by Chatterley Whitfield Collieries Limited, and when it closed in November 1904, its landsale wharf alongside the Leek Road at Joiners Square (known as Botterslow Wharf) was retained as an outlet for Whitfield coal. Because of this, the colliery company had running powers for their engines over the NSR, and were able to move their own traffic between the colliery and Botteslow. The wharf closed 30 July 1948, although the running of the colliery locomotives over the main line had ceased early in LMS days.

On 1 January 1895 the NSR acquired the LAG&BR, and the Act giving it the powers to do so also enabled the company to close and abandon about 20 chains of the route between Adderley Green and Park Hall. Thereafter it was operated as two quite separate branches. This was the 'summit' section, where the line climbed from both ends, by similar gradients, making it a difficult line to work as a through route. To all intents and purposes therefore, it had never been operated as such and the NSR wasted no time in abandoning the summit section, as provided for in the Act. It closed on 14 May 1895, and the track was sub-

Biddulph Valley line leaving Stoke Junction on 6 September 1953, looking south-east towards Pratts Sidings – the line did a loop here to head due north at Fenton Manor. Note Pratts Sidings signal box, the bridge under City Road (the main thoroughfare from Stoke to Fenton and Longton), NSR McKenzie & Holland signals and the locomotive shed yard to left. (FW Shuttleworth)

sequently lifted, although the land remained in railway ownership until after the final closure of the entire LAG&BR system.

There were never any passenger trains on this line, and traffic was almost exclusively coal, although a truncated section of the Hulme Valley Branch did later see some stone working from adjacent quarries. When Park Hall Colliery closed in December 1962, traffic on the Millfield Junction section largely ceased, although some continued for a few months, serving a landsale wharf at Meir Hay. It finally closed 12 December 1963.

The other end of the line did not last much longer and when Mossfield Colliery closed in May 1963, traffic almost ceased – the section closed officially 6 July 1964 – and Botteslow Junction signal box was abolished 10 January 1965. The Hulme Valley branch had been considerably cut back, west of the Bucknall to Weston Coyney road, when Hulme Colliery closed in 1903. The remaining stub closed at the same time as the main route. It had latterly served as a loading dock for lorries bringing stone from nearby quarries. Both this branch, and the line into Adderley Green Colliery, faced Millfield Junction, so that after the line was severed as a through route, the last few chains at the Botteslow end served as a back shunt for these two junctions.

As well as large Robert Heath-owned collieries and iron works at both Ford Green and Black Bull, the Biddulph Valley line served Chatterley Whitfield Col-

liery at Chell, although this colliery company had its own private line heading west to Tunstall. It connected here with the Pinnox Branch and so only local traffic, heading south, went via the Biddulph Valley line (most went north, for ship-ment via either Birkenhead or Liverpool). There were also private branches north of Chell and west of the line, to serve the Chell coal and ironstone pits, the Turnhurst pits and the Wedgwood and Packmoor pits. In its heyday, the Biddulph Valley line was a very busy one, with plentiful mineral traffic. As well as the Whitfield private trains to Botteslow, the colliery company ran its own workmen's services to Congleton, and Heath's its own mineral traffic both between their various sites, and to and from Congleton Brunswick Wharf.

As the pits and ironworks closed – the latter in 1928 – the importance of the route decreased. The first NSR branch line passenger service to be ended under LMS ownership was that beyond Milton Junction, on 11 July 1927. Passenger trains between Stoke and Milton Junction continued, and onwards to Leek, but this service was discontinued from 7 May 1956. However, some excursions continued to serve the Leek line stations,

as well as Ford Green (beyond Milton Junction on the Biddulph Valley line) and Bucknall & Northwood, until the early 1960s. The main line however, was closed in sections:

Congleton Upper Junction - Congleton Lower Junction 1 December 1963
Brunswick Wharf - Heath Junction 15 January 1969
Heath Junction - Ford Green
(rail traffic ceased at Victoria Colliery) January 1976
Ford Green - Milton Junction (closure of Norton Colliery) June 1977

The section Stoke Junction to Milton Junction and onwards to Leek Brook Junction remains in situ unused by any regular traffic since 1989, against the possible reintroduction of stone traffic from Caldon Quarry.

The Biddulph Valley line stations were at Fenton Manor (opened 1 October 1889); Bucknall (& Northwood from August 1861); Ford Green (& Smallthorne from 1890); Chell Halt (opened 3 November 1890); Black Bull; Knypersley Halt (opened October 1914); Gillow Heath (Biddulph from May 1897); Mossley Halt (opened September 1919 - closed c/1925). The line was originally single track beyond Berry Hill and doubled in sections: to Ford Green 1867; to Chell 1 October 1883; to Heath Junction December 1883 – it remained single beyond there. In reverse order, it was singled Heath Junction to Ford Green 19 February 1967.

This picture shows the site of Ford Green Ironworks slag tips, looking north along the Biddulph Valley line on 15 March 1962. Ford Green Yard signal box can just be discerned in the middle distance. This controlled the colliery sidings, the colliery itself being out of sight behind the dirt tip to the right. Wagons in the sidings are awaiting loading either at Norton, or other collieries along the line. The water in the right foreground is the remnant of the Foxley Branch Canal, a branch of the Caldon Canal dating from about 1800. It was built to serve the coal and ironstone workings here, and fell out of use after the railway was built. This is the section of line that suffered from severe flooding as the track sunk due to mining subsidence – working trains through flood water was such a problem when diesels were first introduced, that steam had to continue on this section for a couple of months after the official closure of Stoke shed, until the Civil Engineer completed permanent repairs. Also just about discernible to the left of the line and in the extreme distance, is the embankment that had taken the private colliery line to Nettlebank Wharf at Smallthorne. This had earlier served coal workings both there and adjacent to Holden Lane, and latterly obviated horses and carts having to take the coal for land sale up the steep gradient of Ford Green Road (Smallthorne Bank). It closed in 1957. (FW Shuttleworth)

Train of loaded coal wagons coming off Norton Colliery on 1 May 1967, with an ex-LMS 8F in charge. Note NSR McKenzie & Holland ground disc signal in the 'six foot', a rare survivor by this date. (MG Fell)

By the time this photograph was taken on 1st May 1967, the former up line was out of use, and here can be seen a Standard Class 4 with coal from Victoria Colliery and sand from Biddulph, regaining the up line south of Ford Green. Note the former up line in the foreground of this view taken from the signal box. In the distance can just be seen the top of Ford Green Yard signal box and the supports of the bridge that took the private colliery line over the Biddulph Valley line to serve Nettlebank Wharf at Smallthorne. (M G Fell)

Train of coal empties climbing the 1 in 90 from Ford Green towards Chatterley Whitfield Colliery at Chell, 1 May 1967. By this time the former up line in the foreground was out of use, the down line serving for traffic in both directions. The engine is Stoke-allocated 8F No 48768. (MG Fell)

Black Bull on 18 February 1967, looking north towards the summit of the almost continuous 1 in 90 from Ford Green. The box was permanently switched out by this date, the last day of double track working. It was put out of use and all signals taken away the following day. Notice remains of station beyond – just the buildings are left – and the Victoria Colliery old dirt tips to right. The overhead ropeway took the dirt to the newer tips at Brown Lees, out of sight to the left. There used to be a rail connection here with Brown Lees Colliery and the formation of this can just be made out on the left of the line. The bridge over the line beyond the ropeway carries the private mineral railway between the colliery and the Birchenwood complex at Kidsgrove. There were iron-works and forges here until 1928, the colliery not closing until August 1982. However, rail traffic had ceased sometime earlier on 24 January 1976, with the much reduced output of the pit going by road. At this time the Biddulph Valley line was cut back to Chell. (Allan C Baker)

Class 5 No.45395 of Springs Branch, with the Saturday morning Congleton Brunswick Wharf to Warrington and St Helens sand train, passing the former station at Biddulph, on 18 February 1967. The gates are being operated by the train crew, for by this time this section of the line was operating under the 'one engine in steam' beyond Heath Junction. Former station buildings to left and goods shed to right. The sand was taken to Brunswick Wharf by road from several local quarries and was used in the Lancashire glass industry. This photograph and another two I took at the same time, are the only views I have ever seen of a train at Biddulph. I never managed to catch a train here on any other occasion! (Allan C Baker)

Congleton Lower Junction on 12 April 1962 with 4F No.44393 (a long term Stoke shed engine) returning from Brunswick Wharf with a sand train for Stoke. The line on the right is the connecting spur to the Upper Junction and the NSR main line to Macclesfield can be seen on the embankment in the background – view looks north. The connecting spur was taken out of use 1 December 1963 and thereafter all traffic had to go via Stoke – a long way if it was headed in the Manchester direction! (FW Shuttleworth)

Stanier Class 5 2-6-0 No.42956 of Crewe South, running light and approaching Milton Station past the goods yard there on 13 June 1953. This is on the single line section of the Milton Junction to Leek Brook Junction line and in the right background can be seen the buildings of the British Aluminium Company Works at Milton. The nature of this working is not known, but in view of the special C830 reporting number on the headboard, the engine is presumably going to Leek to work a special of some sort. (FW Shuttleworth)

Milton Station on 13 June 1953, with the 4.30pm Leek to Stoke local passenger train calling, hauled by Stoke's No.42665 running bunker first. The principal station buildings here were at road level, to the right of the picture, on the overbridge rather than on the platform. The coach next to the engine is of Lancashire & Yorkshire Railway origin. This line lost its passenger service on 7 May 1956 and, although there is currently no traffic, the track remains in situ. (FW Shuttleworth)

CHAPTER NINE
THE CHURNET VALLEY LINE AND BRANCHES

The Churnet Valley line, 27 miles and 54 chains of double track from North Rode just south of Macclesfield, to Uttoxeter on the line from Stoke to Derby and Burton-on Trent, was built under powers conferred in one of the three Acts of Parliament of 1846, by which the NSR was incorporated. The line, which opened throughout on 13 July 1849, followed the valley of the River Churnet from Leek to just south of Rocester, where it flowed into the River Dove. Between North Rode and Rushton, the line followed the course of the River Dane. From Froghall to Uttoxeter, it assumed much of the course of the Uttoxeter Canal, abandoned under powers in the Parliamentary Act to build the railway.

A very scenic route, passing through some beautiful countryside, it served the market town of Leek, roughly half-way along its length. The line climbed sharply after a dip at Bosley, one and a half miles from North Rode at 1 in 130 to Rudyard, and then descended all the way to Uttoxeter, with tunnels at Leek (500 yards), Cheddleton (550 yards) and Oakamoor (490 yards). At Rudyard the line followed the north shore of Rudyard Lake, a local beauty spot of some repute,

actually a reservoir constructed to feed the Caldon Canal, and via it the summit section of the Trent & Mersey Canal. Both these canals were acquired by the NSR under powers in its original Acts of Incorporation.

On 31 May 1852 a branch was opened from Rocester, five miles from Uttoxeter, six miles and 65 chains to Ashbourne; on 1 November 1867, another branch (six miles and 46 chains) opened from Milton Junction on the Biddulph Valley line to Cheddleton – one and a half miles south of Leek. In this way the Pottery towns were given direct access to Leek. On 4 August 1899, the LNWR extended its line from Parsley Hay, thirteen miles via Hartington, Alsop en le Dale and Thorpe Cloud, to Ashbourne – another very scenic route. This necessitated revised arrangements at Ashbourne, and the old NSR terminal was closed (it was retained for goods), and a new joint station opened. The NSR also had an engine shed at Ashbourne. By an 1867 agreement the LNWR enjoyed running powers over the entire NSR network; both companies commenced through running between Buxton and Derby, the NSR operating some of the trains to and from Buxton.

Last of the lines in this section was the Leek, Caldon Low & Hartington Light Railway, built under the provisions of the Light Railway Act of 1896. This was part of an ambitious scheme to open up the Manifold Valley, and at the same time the Leek & Manifold Valley Light Railway was promoted. The line left the Churnet Valley line at Leek Brook Junction (where a triangular arrangement was introduced so that trains could enter and leave the branch in either direction) and ran 8 miles 68 chains to Waterhouses with some pretty severe gradients – five miles of 1 in 45/59, from Leek Brook to beyond Ipstones, albeit in favour of loaded trains from Caldon Quarry. It then descended at 1 in 61 for over a mile, with another mile and a half at 1 in 40 to the terminus at Waterhouses. Here connection was made with the 2ft. 6in. gauge Leek & Manifold Valley Light Railway. There was a 61 chain branch, from Caldon Low Junction to serve the company's Caldon Quarry (officially Froghall Quarry, but always colloquially known as Caldon Low). The standard gauge light railway was opened to Ipstones on 15 June 1905 and onwards to Waterhouses and the Quarry on 1 July

Endon Station, looking towards Leek on 29 October 1966. Despite passenger services ceasing in 1956, excursions continued to call here during the 'Stoke Wakes' holidays until the early 1960s. As can be seen the platforms were staggered and from here to Leek Brook Junction the line was double track. (Allan C Baker)

the same year. These lines had a lingering demise, with Leek-Waterhouse losing its passenger services on 30 September 1935, the Leek & Manifold narrow gauge section having closed completely 12 March 1934. The section between Caldon Junction and Waterhouses closed completely on 1 March 1943. This left the line between Leek Brook and the Quarry, and local goods services on this section were withdrawn from 4 May 1964, leaving only the stone traffic. This continued, largely as ballast for railway purposes, until the quarry contract to supply to the railway ceased in 1989. Surprisingly, the line still remains in place, together with the section between Leek Brook and Milton Junction, and the Biddulph Valley line from there to Stoke, but it is in an markedly moribund state today.

Ashbourne lost its passenger services on 1 November 1954, and the local passenger service between Stoke and Leek ceased on 7 May two years later. The passenger service via the LNWR route to Ashbourne from Buxton ceased at the same time as the NSR one, but specials continued to visit Ashbourne, as well as intermediate stations between there and Parsley Hay, almost until the final closure, which came on 1 June 1964. The LNWR section finished a little earlier, on 7 October the previous year.

The Churnet Valley line itself lost its through passenger trains on 7 November 1960, but a limited workmen's service continued between Leek and Uttoxeter, principally for Bolton's copper works at Froghall and Oakamoor. The line between North Rode and Leek closed completely on 15 June 1964, and between Oakamoor and Uttoxeter on 4 January 1965. This left the section between Leek Brook and Oakamoor to serve the British Industrial Sand Company Quarry, and this remained open until the traffic ceased on 30 August 1988. However, like the Caldon Section, and the line to Stoke, the track was left in situ. It was sold on 20 March 1995, to the Cheddleton-based preservation society, the North Staffordshire Railway Company (1978) Limited. This organisation and the Churnet Valley Railway (1992) plc, have grown out of the North Staffordshire Railway Society, which was formed in about 1974, and developed operations in the old station yard at Cheddleton. They always had aspirations to run trains over the remaining section of the line and, from the summer of 1998, have done so between Leek Brook and Consall – two and a half miles south of Cheddleton. Later, it is hoped to extend further south to the site of the sand quarry at Oakamoor. It would be nice, and very much better financially I suspect, if the line could be relaid and trains extended further southwards to Alton, where they could add to the attractions of Alton Towers and encompass one of the most beautiful parts of the valley.

The 3.44pm Macclesfield to Uttoxeter local passenger pausing at Cliffe Park Halt, on the Churnet Valley line, 30 September 1959. The train is hauled by Fowler tank No.42363 from Macclesfield shed which, unusually, is running bunker first. Turning facilities did exist at both Macclesfield and Uttoxeter. Until 1 April 1926, this halt was known as Rudyard Lake. As the same time the next station south, previously called plain Rudyard, became Rudyard Lake. It was located at the extreme northern end of the lake. (Michael Mensing)

Wall Grange & Longsdon Station on 29 June 1953 with a Leek to Stoke local passenger train calling, headed by Stoke Class 4 Fowler tank No.42360. Originally single track, the section between Endon and Leek Brook was doubled in two stretches, Leek Brook to Wall Grange on 7 August 1909, and onwards to Endon on 23 March 1910. Presumably this is the reason why the down side platform (to the left) is of wooden construction, being of much later origin – note the small goods yard to the left. The chimney and tower on the skyline mark the Staffordshire County Council St Edward's Mental Hospital; the building below the trees to the extreme left is the Wall Grange pumping station of the Staffordshire Potteries Water Board. Longsdon was a good ¾ mile from the station and it was a stiff climb out of the valley through which both the railway and the earlier Caldon Canal passed. (FW Shuttleworth)

Rudyard Lake station on 3 September 1954, showing the down platform and signal box, the latter unusually situated on the platform. This was a popular destination for excursions, both from the Pottery towns and further afield. The NSR promoted the lake extensively as a pleasure resort, as they owned it. Actually it was a man made reservoir built as a feeder to the Caldon Canal, which in turn fed the summit section of the Trent & Mersey Canal. Both canals were owned by the NSR. (Late Dr JR Hollick)

Leek Brook Junction, originally Cheddleton Junction, in the late summer of 1966. The Churnet Valley line is to the left, Stoke line to the right. Leek Brook Station, opened by the LMS on I January 1929, was just out of sight around the corner on the Stoke line. The Churnet Valley line penetrated the high ground in the background by the 550 yard Cheddleton Tunnel. The sand between the rails betrays one of the line's staple traffic flows at this date, sand from the quarry at Oakamoor usually destined for the glass industry around St Helens. (Allan C Baker)

Train of railway ballast en-route from Caldon Quarry, on the Leek Caldon Low & Hartington Light Railway. This was the only section of the NSR, apart from the narrow gauge Leek & Manifold Valley Light Railway, built under the powers of the Light Railways Act. It opened completely on 1 July 1905 and is still in situ between Leek Brook and the quarry, albeit not in use. Here is Stoke 4F 0-6-0 No.44393 on 2 April 1959 leaving Bradnop and heading towards Leek Brook Junction down the steep three miles of 1 in 45 – the train would be completely vacuum fitted. The remains of Bradnop Station platform can just be seen behind the brake van. There had been a passing loop here, the branch being single track – it lost its passenger services on 30 September 1935. (FW Shuttleworth)

Panoramic view taken on 15 March 1962 from above the southern portal of the 490 yard Oakamoor Tunnel, looking south along the Churnet Valley line. The level crossing gates were hand worked in view of their distance from the signal box. The sidings to the left served Thomas Bolton's copper works – there was another, more recent Works at Froghall. Notice station beyond and NSR crossing keeper's house in left foreground. (FW Shuttleworth)

A delightful view of Alton Towers station (plain Alton until January 1954) on 19 August 1961. By this date the Churnet Valley had lost its through passenger services, but a limited service ran between Uttoxeter and Leek, principally to serve the needs of the workers at the two copper works of Thomas Bolton & Sons Limited at Froghall and Oakamoor. Here we see the 11.18am Uttoxeter to Leek, calling at Alton and hauled by Fowler Class 4 tank No.42323. The engines that worked these trains travelled 'light' to and from Leek or Uttoxeter from Stoke shed, as necessary. The station buildings at Alton were built to the designs of the Architect AW Pugin, well known in the period as he had also been responsible for parts of nearby Alton Towers, the seat of the Earls' of Shrewsbury. (Michael Mensing)

Rocester signal box on 28 March 1965, after the line had closed. This was the junction of the six mile 65 chain branch to Ashbourne, opened 31 May 1852. It lost its passenger services on 1 November 1954. The factory building to left is part of the JCB plant (well known builders of earth moving equipment) built on the trackbed of the Ashbourne branch, which closed completely on 1 June 1964. (FW Shuttleworth)

Norbury & Ellastone, the first station from Rocester on the Ashbourne branch, in 1957. A passing loop was situated here, just beyond the platforms (the view is towards Ashbourne). Enjoy the splendid original NSR McKenzie & Holland lower quadrant signals, with the down home and up starter on the same post. (Late Dr JR Hollick)

Appendix

Locomotive Allocations
NOVEMBER 1945

STOKE
Stanier Class 3 2-6-2T
122; 123; 125; 126; 127; 128; 156; 157.
Fowler Class 4 2-6-4T
2305; 2306; 2315; 2316; 2324; 2343; 2344; 2345; 2358; 2363; 2364; 2375; 2376; 2391.
Stanier Class 4 2-6-4T
2430; 2467; 2468; 2542; 2543; 2564; 2569; 2575; 2584; 2592; 2593; 2598; 2603; 2605; 2609; 2628; 2660; 2661; 2662; 2663; 2664; 2665; 2666; 2667; 2668; 2669; 2670; 2671; 2672; 2673; 2674; 2675; 2676; 2677.
Fowler Class 4 0-6-0
4067; 4093; 4310; 4343; 4363; 4373; 4377; 4378; 4380; 4381; 4383; 4388; 4391; 4393; 4448; 4478; 4489; 4496; 4498; 4499; 4500; 4502; 4503; 4504; 4508.
Stanier Class 5 4-6-0
5278; 5324; 5498.
Fowler Class 3 0-6-0T
7320; 7338; 7370; 7587; 7596; 7599; 7609; 7610; 7647; 7648; 7658.
Ex LNWR Cauliflower Class 2 0-6-0
28442; 28460; 28464.
Total 98

ALSAGER
Stanier Class 3 2-6-2T
78.
Fowler Class 4 2-6-4T
2309; 2348.
Stanier Class 4 2-6-4T
2471; 2611.
Fowler Class 4 0-6-0
4301; 4348; 4450; 4451; 4452; 4497.
Fowler Class 3 0-6-0T
7392; 7595; 7661; 7662.
Total 15

UTTOXETER
Stanier Class 3 2-6-2T
85; 86; 87.
Fowler Class 4 2-6-4T
2303; 2304; 2346.
Stanier Class 4 2-6-4T
2431.
Fowler Class 4 0-6-0
4307.
Total 8

MACCLESFIELD
Fowler Class 3 2-6-2T
51; 55.
Fowler Class 4 2-6-4T
2319; 2347; 2355; 2356; 2369; 2382.
Total 8 - Grand Total 129.

FEBRUARY 1953
STOKE
Stanier Class 3 2-6-2T
40143; 40202; 40205.
Fairburn Class 4 2-6-4T
42063; 42233; 42234; 42235; 42236.
Fowler Class 4 2-6-4T
42303; 42323; 42343; 42344; 42348; 42349; 42360; 42364; 42375; 42378.
Stanier Class 4 2-6-4T
42431; 42440; 42443; 42445; 42458; 42494; 42543; 42567; 42590; 42593; 42600; 42603; 42605; 42609; 42667; 42668; 42671; 42672; 42675.
Fowler Class 4 0-6-0
43915; 43980; 44068; 44074; 44077; 44093; 44308; 44309; 44310; 44353; 44354; 44358; 44369; 44373; 44374; 44375; 44377; 44378; 44380; 44383; 44385;

44388; 44393; 44388; 44393; 44405; 44421; 44455; 44478; 44484; 44496; 44498; 44499; 44500; 44502; 44507; 44508; 44513; 44548; 44596.
Stanier Class 5 4-6-0
44871; 45149; 45257; 45278; 45324; 45381.
Fowler Class3 0-6-0T
47281; 47344; 47370; 47380; 47472; 47587; 47596; 47599; 47609; 47610; 47647; 47648; 47658.
Ex LNWR Cauliflower Class 2 0-6-0
58376; 58382.
Total 98

ALSAGER
Stanier Class 4 2-6-4T
42447; 42471; 42611.
Fowler Class 4 0-6-0
44063; 44079; 44125; 44126; 44300; 44342; 44386; 44450; 44452; 44453; 44503.
Fowler Class 3 0-6-0T
47445; 47595; 47598; 47662; 47633.
Total 19

UTTOXETER
Stanier Class 3 2-6-2T
40086; 40156.
Fowler Class 4 2-6-4T
42358.
Stanier Class 4 2-6-4T
42665.
Fowler Class 4 0-6-0
44307; 44504.
Total 6

MACCLESFIELD
Fowler Class 4 2-6-4T
42355; 42356; 42357;42369;. 42381; 42382; 42386.
Total 7 - Grand Total 130.

APRIL 1960
STOKE
Fowler Class 4 2-6-4T
42315; 42323; 42344; 42346; 42362; 42378; 42420; 42421.
Stanier Class 4 2-6-4T
42443; 42454; 42459; 42464; 42543; 42590; 42593; 42600; 42603; 42609; 42663; 42667; 42668; 42670; 42671; 42672.
Hughes/Fowler 'Crab' Class 5 2-6-0
42777; 42782; 42811; 42888; 42891.
Stanier Class 5 2-6-0
42920; 42929.
Fowler Class 4 0-6-0
44068; 44074; 44115; 44186; 44246; 44271; 44307; 44309; 44310; 44344; 44358; 44377; 44393; 44395; 44424; 44432; 44455; 44478; 44484; 44499; 44500; 44508; 44536; 44548; 44593.
Stanier Class 5 4-6-0
45044; 45060.
Ivatt Class 2 2-6-0
46429; 46430.
Fowler Class 3 0-6-0T
47344; 47380; 47451; 47587; 47596; 47609; 47648; 47658.
BR Standard Diesel-Electric Shunting Locomotives - 350HP 0-6-0
D3798; D3799; D3800; D3801; D3802; D3866.
Total Steam 68 - Diesel 6

ALSAGER
Fowler Class 4 0-6-0
44061; 44063; 44067; 44079; 44125; 44342; 44349; 44352; 44354; 44386; 44405; 44450; 44452.
Fowler Class 3 0-6-0T
47401;47445;47598;47606.
Stanier Class 5 4-6-0
45131.
Total 18

Uttoxeter
Fowler Class 4 2-6-4T
42358; 42375.
Stanier Class 4 2-6-4T
42665; 42605.
Fowler Class 4 0-6-0
44355.
Total 5

MACCLESFIELD
Fowler Class 4 2-6-4T
42318; 42347; 42348;.42355; 42363; 42382.
Total 6 - Grand Total Steam 97 - Diesel 6.

OCTOBER 1963
STOKE
Fairburn Class 4 2-6-4T
42066; 42160.
Fowler Class 4 2-6-4T
42224; 42226; 42381.
Stanier Class 4 2-6-4T
42542;.42590; 42609; 42663; 42667.
Stanier Class 5 2-6-0
42948; 42949; 42953; 42956; 42959; 42961; 42963; 42977; 42980.
Ivatt Class 3 2-6-0
43003; 43019; 43112; 43115; 43118.
Fowler Class 4 -0-6-0
44068; 44079; 44115; 44242; 44310; 44342; 44344; 44349; 44354; 44395; 44424; 44432; 44499; 44500; 44536; 44548.
Stanier Class 5 4-6-0
45003; 45020; 45037; 45060; 45074; 45132; 45146; 45191; 45240; 45241; 45257; 45276; 45350; 45387; 45395; 45446.
Fowler Class 3 0-6-0T
47280; 47587; 47596; 47609; 47664.
Stanier Class 8 2-8-0
48248; 48453; 48516; 48548; 48555.
Standard Class 4 4-6-0
75014; 75018; 75030; 75031; 75034; 75036; 75037; 75040; 75053; 75056; 75062.
Standard Class 4 2-6-0
76020; 76022; 76023; 76047; 76051; 76075; 76085; 76086; 76088.
Standard Class 2 2-6-0
78017; 78056.
Standard Diesel Shunting-Electric Locomotives- 350HP 0-6-0
D3800; D3801; D4108; D4109; D4110; D3866.
Total Steam 88 - Diesel 6

UTTOXETER
Fairburn Class 4 2-6-4T
42069.
Stanier Class 4 2-6-4T
42564; 42605.
Fowler Class 4 0-6-0
44048; 44355.
Fowler Class 3 0-6-0T
47628.
Total 6 - Grand Total Steam 94 - Diesel 6

DMU ALLOCATION AT COCKSHUTE DECEMBER 1964

Driving Motor Coaches (Three Car Units, Birmingham Railway Carriage & Wagon - later Class 104).-
M50439/40/2-71;.M50491/2/4-9; M50500-12/14-23.
Intermediate Trailers - M59147/8/50-79.
Driving Motor Coaches (Two car Units 50411/ 56164 Park Royal, remainder Birmingham Railway Carriage & Wagon) - M50411; M50536-8.
Driving Trailers - M56164; M56179-81.
Parcels Van -(Cravens) M55999.

ALLOCATION AND DISPOSAL AT STOKE FROM JANUARY 1967 TO CLOSURE

Ivatt Class 3 2-6-0
43001 to Crewe South 8/1967
43002 to Workington 8/1967
43007 to Crewe South 8/1967
43021 to Crewe South 6/1967
43088 to Crewe South 6/1967
43112 to Crewe South 8/1967
43115 withdrawn 6/1967

Stanier Class 5 4-6-0
44661 allocated 4/1967; withdrawn 8/1967

44682 to Springs Branch

9/1967
44713 to Lostock Hall 6/1967
44770 to Carlisle Kingmoor

3/1967
44805 allocated 4/1967; to Crewe South 8/1967
44840 allocated 4/1967; to

Birkenhead 8/1967
44859 to Birkenhead 8/1967
44860 withdrawn 1/1967
44876 allocated 4/1967; to Birkenhead 8/1967
44985 to Springs Branch

5/1967
45003 withdrawn 6/1967
45038 to Lostock Hall 6/1967
45050 withdrawn 8/1967
45052 allocated 4/1967 to

Crewe South 8/1967
45060 withdrawn 3/1967
45191 withdrawn 7/1967
45240 withdrawn 1/1967
45241 to Crewe South 8/1967
45268 to Springs Branch 5/1967
45270 to Crewe South 8/1967
45276 withdrawn 1/1967
45292 to Birkenhead 8/1967
45299 to Birkenhead 8/1967
45302 withdrawn 7/1967
45308 withdrawn 8/1967
45350 to Springs Branch

3/1967
45405 to Birkenhead 8/1967

Stanier Class 8 2-8-0
48012 to Edge Hill 6/1967
48018 to Crewe South 3/1967
48061 allocated 3/1967; to Rose Grove 9/1967
48085 to Northwich 6/1967
48110 withdrawn 6/1967
48128 allocated 3/1967;

withdrawn 6/1967
48131 withdrawn 6/1967
48256 withdrawn 5/1967
48343 withdrawn 2/1967
48364 to Crewe South 8/1967
48368 to Newton Heath 8/1967
48375 to Rose Grove 9/1967
48402 allocated 3/1967; to Crewe South 8/1967
48453 to Patricroft 3/1967
48522 withdrawn 8/1967
48548 to Crewe South 3/1967
48729 allocated 3/1967; to Crewe South 8/1967
48697 allocated 6/1967; to

Heaton Mersey 8/1967
48767 to Crewe South 3/1967
48768 to Heaton Mersey

8/1967
Standard Class 4 4-6-0
75002 allocated 6/1967; withdrawn 8/1967
75006 allocated 6/1967;

withdrawn 8/1967
75013 allocated 5/1967; withdrawn 8/1967
75018 withdrawn 6/1967
75029 allocated 6/1967; withdrawn 8/1967
75030 to Tebay 6/1967

75032 to Tebay 5/1967
75034 to Carnforth 6/1967
75035 to Tebay 6/1967
75037 to Tebay 5/1967
75040 to Tebay 5/1967
75046 allocated 5/1967;

withdrawn 8/1967
75047 allocated 6/1967; withdrawn 8/1967
75052 allocated 6/1967;

withdrawn 8/1967
75055 allocated 5/1967; withdrawn 6/1967
75064 to Aintree 5/1967
75071 allocated 6/1967; withdrawn 8/1967
Total 52 at 1/1967 - 35 at closure 8/1967.

Photo below. **A self explanatory notice at Congleton Brunswick Wharf, photographed on 12 April 1968, announcing the then recent closure of the facilities there. (Allan C Baker).**

Tunnels on NSR

Tunnel	Length (yards)	Open	Closed
Harecastle North	130	9/10/1848	Opened Out
Harecastle Middle	180	9/10/1848	27/6/1966
Harecasle South	1763	9/10/1848	27/6/1966
Meir	847	7/8/1848	Still Open
Newcastle (Short)	96	6/9/1852	8/3/1966
Newcastle (Long)	650	6/9/1852	8/3/1966
Silverdale	686	1/2/1870	Still Open
Keele (Long)	316	1/2/1870	Still Open
Keele (Short)	33	1/2/1870	Still Open
Cobridge	310	1/11/1873	3/1/1966
Kidsgrove	88	15/11/1875	1/1976
Oakamoor	490	13/7/1849	4/1/1965
Cheddleton	550	13/7/1849	Still in Use
Leek	500	13/7/1849	15/6/1964
Cheadle	900	1/1/1901	26/11/1933

The BRITISH RAILWAYS BOARD Regret THAT IT HAS BEEN FOUND NECESSARY TO WITHDRAW THE EXISTING FREIGHT FACILITIES FROM CONGLETON (BRUNSWICK WHARF) GOODS DEPOT ON AND FROM MONDAY 1ST. APRIL 1968

ALTERNATIVE FACILITIES ARE AVAILABLE AT THE MAIN CONGLETON GOODS DEPOT EXCEPT FOR COAL CLASS TRAFFIC FOR WHICH ALTERNATIVE FACILITIES ARE AVAILABLE AT KIDSGROVE

British Rail